TWAYNE'S WORLD AUTHORS SERIES
A Survey of the World's Literature

GERMANY

Ulrich Weisstein, Indiana University
EDITOR

Ludwig Thoma

TWAS 494

Ludwig Thoma

LUDWIG THOMA

By BRUNO F. STEINBRUCKNER

The American University

TWAYNE PUBLISHERS

A DIVISION OF G. K. HALL & CO., BOSTON

Library of Congress Cataloging in Publication Data

Steinbruckner, Bruno Friedrich.
Ludwig Thoma.

(Twayne's world authors series ; TWAS 494 : Germany)
Bibliography: p. 149 - 51
Includes indexes.
1. Thoma, Ludwig, 1867 - 1921.   2. Authors, German—20th
century—Biography.   I.   Title.
PT2642.H58Z798   838'.'1209 [B]   78-5282
ISBN 0-8057-6335-X

To
my parents and my wife

Contents

About the Author

Bruno F. Steinbruckner is Professor of German Studies and Chairman of the Department of Language and Foreign Studies at The American University in Washington, D.C. He was born and raised in Linz, Austria, and attended Teacher's Training College there. In 1965 he received his Ph.D. in German Literature and Philology from the University of Innsbruck. Dr. Steinbruckner has been a Consultant in Research at The George Washington University and he held the title of President of The American Goethe Society in Washington, D.C. from 1971 - 1973.

Dr. Steinbruckner's other publications include the book *Dialektographie des Oberen Mühlviertels* published by Elwert Publishing Company in Germany in 1976, articles in scholarly journals such as *The German Quarterly, Monatshefte, Orbis, Muttersprache, Euphorion, Sudetenland* and *Zeitschrift für deutsche Sprache,* and numerous entries in the *Encylcopedic Dictionary of Religion,* 1978.

Preface

Compared with some of his contemporaries, Ludwig Thoma has received very little attention by literary critics. There are only a few books and articles written about him in German, and an even smaller number of studies in English. Fifty years after his death, most of his major works are forgotten. Even devout students of German literature often associate Thoma only with his *Lausbubengeschichten*, thus placing him into the scarce "funny papers" of German cultural history; or they might remember the picture of his coarse-looking face, the pince-nez sitting on his little snub-nose and the gigantic peasant's pipe hanging from his mouth. This is how Thoma used to be portrayed in literary histories. And it is also the stereotyped image prevailing today: a beer-drinking, pipe-smoking, middle-aged Bavarian who, in a nostalgic moment, recalled his lively adolescent years full of boyish intrigues spun against the older generation, but who, eventually, became a faithful subject of the Bavarian king, and who, in all probability, remained a loyal and well-nourished Bavarian until his untimely death, which, it is also assumed, was caused by his overconsumption of beer. This just about completes the slightly "romantic" but erroneous conception of Ludwig Thoma which has emerged over the past decades and which has solidly established itself in Germany and abroad. The conscientious reader of Thoma's works has to ask himself how such a distorted view of the author's personality could have evolved. It is one of the goals of this study to show the reasons for this phenomenal misunderstanding of Ludwig Thoma, and also to correct his hackneyed image.

Half a century after Thoma's death, we have acquired the detachment necessary for an objective assessment of his life and work. Because of the absence of a definitive monograph, it seems necessary to include a biography at the beginning of this study, especially since most of Thoma's works are directly related to persons and places with which he was acquainted. It may also be valuable for the individual eager to obtain a more thorough knowledge of Thoma to receive an explanation of the unique political and cultural situation in which Bavaria found itself during his life span. Although he was much more than a regional Bavarian writer, one would be ill-advised not to see Thoma as a product of his native land, which he embraced with the love of a son for his mother. Few other writers have displayed such deep feelings for their homeland and its people. At the same time, however, he was a merciless critic of empty patriotism and of parochial attitudes.

BRUNO F. STEINBRUCKNER

Chronology

Florence together with several colleagues from the *Simplicissimus* during the spring.

1904 Makes a trip to southern France, northern Africa, and Sicily.

1905 Publication of his first novel, *Andreas Vöst*. Marries Marietta di Rigardo.

1906 Founds the periodical *März*, together with Albert Langen, Hermann Hesse, and Kurt Aram. Serves a six-week prison sentence in Munich / Stadelheim.

1908 Moves into his new house on the "Tuften" in Rottach / Tegernsee. Publication of *Filserbriefe* (Filser Letters) and *Moral* (Morals).

1909 Albert Langen dies.

1910 Publication of *Erster Klasse*, which becomes a big success. Separation from Marietta.

1911 Spends several weeks in Paris during the spring. Publication of *Der Wittiber* (The Widower).

1912 *Magdalena*.

1913 Thoma's best friend, Ignatius Taschner, dies.

1914 August 1, World War I starts. Thoma tries to sign up for military service. Travels to the Western Front as a member of the Red Cross.

1915 Serves as a medic in the Red Cross in France and on the Eastern Front, where he contracts dysentery and is forced to return home.

1916 *Heilige Nacht* (Holy Night).

1917 *Altaich*.

1918 The end of World War I and the collapse of the German *Reich* leaves Thoma deeply depressed. In summer he meets Maidi von Liebermann.

1919 Writes 149 articles of political content for the *Miesbacher Anzeiger*. His deep grief over the fate of Germany continues. He meets Dr. Josef Hofmiller.

1920 Publication of *Der Jagerloisl* and work on *Kaspar Lorinser*.

1921 Works on his last novel, *Der Ruepp*. First signs of severe stomach ailment appear. On August 6, he is operated on in the Red Cross Hospital in Munich. On August 26, he dies in his house on the "Tuften."

CHAPTER 1

Biography

I *Childhood*

L UDWIG Thoma was born on January 21, 1867, in Oberammergau, the site of the famous Passion Play, situated in one of Upper Bavaria's romantic Alpine valleys. Although Ludwig's parents had close family ties to this place, his birth there was merely incidental. His father, Max Thoma, was a royal Bavarian gamekeeper in Vorderriss, a remote little hamlet in the Upper Isar Valley, roughly forty miles east of Oberammergau. During the winter, the forester's house was practically cut off from the outside world, and therefore it was not a suitable place for an expectant mother. Marie, the sister of Ludwig's mother, who was married to a well-to-do publisher in the town of the Passion Play, invited her to stay in their roomy, comfortable house. Although Oberammergau thus became Ludwig's birthplace, he never entered into friendly relations to this village. The reasons are fairly obvious: all his life, Thoma had a strong aversion to organized tourism with its ugly commercial side effects. Just when he was born, Oberammergau began to acquire the dubious fame of an international tourist capital, and this was an important reason for Thoma to avoid it in his adult years. His real home was, and remained, at least in his dreams, for all his life, the forester's house in the Vorderriss and its mysterious environs: the dark mountain forests, the turquoise-green Isar River, and the gray limestone ranges of the northern Alps, as grandiose as they were threatening in their majestic tranquillity. This was the setting in which Ludwig grew up as the fifth of seven children. His father, a tall, blue-eyed man, had served the Bavarian kings for more than twenty years as an official of the royal forest service at several places. Ludwig always spoke about him with sincere respect and admiration; he emphasized his discretion and his equanimity, and praised his superior intelligence.[1]

Most of Thoma's ancestors on the father's side had been foresters: his grandfather, Franz Thoma, was game-manager in the town of Kaufbeuren; his great-grandfather, Josef von Thoma, whose ancestors originated in the area of Waldsassen in Upper Palatine, served as a high official of the forest service in Munich. The family of Ludwig's mother, the Pfeiffers, ran a respectable inn in Oberammergau. His mother's father, the "Schwabenwirt," was known as a man of austere character who talked very little and who tolerated no nonsense in his home. The family's children had to address their parents by the formal "Sie," instead of the more common and familiar "Du." Among the "Schwabenwirt's" guests were such illustrious persons as King Maximilian II of Bavaria.

Katharina Pfeiffer, Ludwig's mother, must have been a lovely young woman who, besides her interest in serious literature (she read such books as Goethe's *Werther* and Stifter's *Studien*), had the reputation of being an excellent cook. Max Thoma met her when he was stationed in Piesenhausen near Marquartstein, and he made her his wife shortly afterwards. After living in Partenkirchen from 1861 to 1865, the Thoma family, already six members strong, finally settled in the Vorderriss. In spite of the extreme solitude surrounding the place, both parents welcomed the change, mainly for economic reasons: the new post included the free use of some state-owned farmland as a fringe benefit. Considering the modest salary of a royal official in the forest service and the already large family he had to support, the lonely place seemed more attractive than one less remote but lacking the little farm business. But no one among the Thomas knew yet what the Vorderriss would turn out to be, namely a little paradise for both parents and children. Ludwig tells us with great enthusiasm about the miraculous world around him.[2] He remembers the flowing fountain beneath the maple tree in the back of the house with its granite reservoir, where his father used to keep the trout which had been caught in the river. There was also the sawmill down the Isar River, with its shrieking and monotonous sounds, representing the only noise of "modern" civilization in the valley. A special attraction for the boy were the smoking charcoal piles at the foot of the hill below the house. They were serviced by men covered with soot who untiringly climbed up and down on the piles, wielding long sticks. Other dangerous-looking giants were the raftsmen, always busy tying together huge logs with iron clamps, making them ready for rafting down the river. But the children's favorite companions were the father's rangers, all jolly young fellows who never forgot to bring the children some small treasure from their duties in the forest, be it a little pipe fashioned from the bark of a tree, or a peculiar-looking root. One of the rangers, Thomas Bauer, from Lenggries, the next village down the Isar River, later became a friend of Ludwig Thoma, faithfully visiting the family long after old Thoma had died. Once a week the *Lenggrieser Bote* appeared, a peddler with a covered wagon, bringing with him newspapers, letters, packages, and freshly baked bread. He served as the only link to the outside world for the people of the Vorderriss. Especially popular with the Thoma family were the weekly magazines *Über Land und Meer* and the notorious *Gartenlaube*. Aromatic tobacco smoke and the fragrant smell of freshly brewed coffee provided the atmosphere in which the whole family indulged in reading the news and looking at the pictures from the big world outside. Mixed with an almost insatiable curiosity was a certain cozy feeling of security among the family, an assurance that all the turbulent events they read about could not touch the comfortable solitude of the Vorderriss.

Ludwig made his first acquaintance with literature in *Max und Moritz*, by Wilhelm Busch, a book given to him by one of his father's sisters, Thoma's Aunt Theres. Busch's *Max und Moritz*, with illustrations by the author himself (still among the most popular children's books in Germany today), was already then a great success with young and old. It was also Aunt Theres who introduced Ludwig to the world of the stage: one day she arrived with a little puppet theater with which she gave a performance of *Der Freischütz*, the famous opera by Carl Maria von Weber. This event made a deep impression on Ludwig, and he associated Aunt Theres's *Freischütz* performance with the real stage when he stood behind the curtain of the Munich *Hoftheater* listening to rehearsals many years later.

Christmas in the Vorderriss was an unforgettable experience. Weeks in advance the rangers coming home from the forest would report having seen the *Christkind* flying through the wintery landscape on the other side of the mountain. During clear nights, it seemed that bells were ringing in the woods nearby and lights were flashing in the brush. The Christmas gifts were distributed—as is still the tradition all over the South of Germany and Austria—on Christmas Eve. When Ludwig was about five years old, he was allowed to join the family on a Christmas trip to Oberammergau. Riding in a horse-drawn sleigh along the road from Wallgau, he saw for the first time a real town. Until then, he had only known the three houses of the Vorderriss.

As limited as the social life of the Vorderriss was, it was by no means dull. During the deer season, hunting guests arrived, among them the Duke of Coburg, the Duke of Nassau, and many other high officials in the king's service. Such visits were not always sheer pleasure for Thoma's father, since rivalries between the retainers of the visiting nobility usually had a way of ending up in his lap. Often he was blamed for the incompetence and recklessness of others.

South of the nearby Austrian border, right in the middle of the mighty Karwendel Mountains, lies the Franciscan monastery of Hinterriss. Every Sunday, one of the Franciscan fathers came down to the Vorderriss to read the Mass in the little chapel next to the forester's house for the rangers, lumberjacks, and raftsmen in the valley. From time to time an unusually tall man with strikingly beautiful eyes and rich, wavy hair knelt in front of the altar: King Ludwig II of Bavaria. At that time, he had been king for only a few years, and he did not yet show any signs of mental disorder. He felt comfortable in the modest hunting lodge opposite the forester's house on the plateau overlooking the valley. Because of his love for nature, the king was highly esteemed by the people of the Vorderriss. He had no objection to meeting people who worked in the forest, and he frequently talked to the rangers, all of whom were known to him by name. It was already common knowledge that he used the Vorderriss as a hideout whenever he wanted to escape the unpleasant duties of a host to high visitors at the Munich court. While the Austrian emperor or the crown prince of Prussia were visiting him in his capital, he would suddenly disappear from the city, letting his visitors know that he preferred to breathe the mountain air. For the Thoma children, the arrival of the monarch in the "Riss" was a great spectacle: a few hours before the event, a royal courier came to announce the king's coming, after which Mother Thoma and her servants hastily prepared the lodge. Then carriages with supplies, cooks, and servants arrived, and before long the king's party stopped in front of the forester's house. Thoma's father respectfully greeted the monarch, and his wife presented him with a bouquet of Alpine flowers. The king then asked a few questions in a low voice, and soon disappeared into the house. Sometimes, in the middle of the night, the king's servants summoned Ludwig's father to keep the sleepless king company until the morning.

The 1860's were politically eventful years in Germany. The noise of turbulent happenings even reached the remote Vorderriss and disturbed its tranquillity. There was talk about a conflict between Austria and Prussia in which Bavaria would naturally side with Austria. In case of war, almost everybody in the Vorderriss expected the certain defeat of Prussia. After the Prussian victory of 1866, the people were utterly surprised, and many feared for the loss of Bavaria's independence. Thoma's father was a rational man who did not subscribe to the widespread opinion that Bavaria and the other South German States should form a union in order to keep a political balance vis-à-vis an overpowering Prussian influence in Germany. Finally, the Franco-Prussian War of 1870 cleared the air and silenced the voices of separation. In December, when the Prussian troops besieged Paris, the Vorderriss was suddenly cut off from the world by an early blizzard. The rangers fought their way through the snow to Lenggries, and they soon brought back the news that Paris had fallen. Max Thoma and his men celebrated by firing a gun salute in front of the house. Young Ludwig gathered news clippings and pictures dealing with the campaign, and was especially interested in portraits of Prince Otto von Bismarck. In later years, the "Iron Chancellor" became an idol for him, representing the perfect statesman.

When one of the rangers, who had served as a lieutenant in the artillery during the war, came back from Paris, he brought several trophies, among them a French cuirass and several Chassepot rifles which Max Thoma, himself an expert in weaponry, tested thoroughly. From his father, Ludwig inherited an attachment to handsome weapons.

The beginning of the seventies brought an intensive discussion of the papal dogma of infallibility. In Bavaria, it led to the formation of the Old Catholic Church, a sect which openly rejected the new dogma. A wave of heated public dispute swept through the towns and villages of Bavaria, but did not reach the Vorderriss. Thoma's father could not understand the sudden emergence of spiritual conflicts in the minds of some people, and his wife stuck to her conviction that one should take the good and beautiful aspects of religion as they are and refrain from criticizing the rest. To her, Christianity also meant tolerance of other people's beliefs. A person of similar principles, but a bit more resolute in character, was "the old Viktor," her housemaid and the family's "factotum." "Viktor," whose real name was Viktoria Pröbstl, joined the Thoma household when Ludwig was only two years old, and died thirty-four years later in Ludwig's presence. The daughter of the mayor of Schongau in Upper Bavaria, "the old Viktor" (a nickname Thoma invented for her) was a spinster in her thirties when she accepted the post with the Thoma family. She proved to be such an efficient and at the same time softhearted person, that she soon became indispensable. She honored the affection shown to her with lifelong loyalty. Long after Thoma's mother had died, "old Viktor" reigned over Ludwig's modest household in Dachau near Munich, where he began his career as a country lawyer. "Viktor" was one of those countless true souls who served in German households all their lives, filling by no means merely the position of maid or kitchen help, but becoming a member of the family. She had a definite aversion to repression and tyranny, and she harbored a constant suspicion against novelties which, in her opinion, generally had a way of bringing oppression with them. Although she was endowed with a cheerful nature, she sometimes fell into spells of self-pity during which she would copy sentimental poems into her diary. One of her favorite pastimes was discussing belletristic literature, at which occasions she could boast with her knowledge.

Among the many hunting guests who came to the Vorderriss, only a few became real friends of the family: Duke Ludwig; the Württembergian cabinet minister, von Varnbühler; Count von Pappenheim, who was possessed by an extraordinary, almost comical passion for hunting; and, finally, Thoma's favorite visitor, Colonel Count Tattenbach, who was associated with the Bavarian gun works at Ansbach. The colonel, a short fellow with enormous eyebrows, was very popular with the children. Although he was a man of few words, he must have possessed the rare gift of making those around him comfortable by his mere presence and a few well-aimed jokes. He had a reputation as a skillful hunter even among the rangers, who were generally skeptical of nonprofessionals, the so-called *Sonntagsjäger* (Sunday hunters). An easy way to get the colonel started was to ask about his latest kill. To such a question he would respond by elaborating about tracking, about a good shot, and about securing the kill. While talking over a pipe and a hot cup of coffee, he actually seemed to live through these events a second time. Count Tattenbach was one of the few acquaintances of the family who actively aided Thoma's mother after the death of her husband.

Probably the most aggravating part of the forester's life in the

Vorderriss was the never-ending "war" with the poachers. In these times, perfectly good citizens who would have never thought of committing a crime suddenly turned into ruthless killers. While the rangers were feared and hated by the lawbreakers, the forester himself was respected as a fair man. He arrested the poachers, but treated the wounded and fed them before they were brought in for confinement. The guerrilla-type actions finally came to an end after the implementation of the new federal penal code (*Reichsstrafgesetzbuch*), which clearly spelled out the punishment for the crime of poaching.

As everything in human life, the dreamlike existence in the Vorderriss had to come to an end. It was probably concern for the education of his children that made Max Thoma apply for a new position in the forest service, but it may also have been his weakening health. On the sixteenth of August, 1873, an official letter from his superiors in Munich notified him that his request for transfer had been granted and that he was to report to his new assignment as a royal park-keeper in Forstenried, near Munich. Since he had been given advance notice of the content of this letter, he had had his farm implements auctioned off a few days before. A farewell shooting match in honor of the departing forester provided the last memorable event of the final weeks at the Vorderriss.

As the two wagons carrying the family belongings jolted slowly northeast on the narrow dirt road, young Ludwig could hardly know that his childhood paradise was lost forever. He was soon to discover that he would never long for anything more than for this little piece of land and the people he had known there, living together not entirely without problems, but in a kind of medieval symbiosis. It was a world full of simple beauty and clarity, a remote island far from the artificiality and harmful complexity of human civilization. For Thoma, it had provided the ultimate state of happiness.

In his adult years, Ludwig Thoma never tired of trying to recreate his own "Vorderriss," while at the same time being aware of the futility of such attempts. In examining the floor plans of the "Tuften," his beloved mansion near Rottach on the Tegernsee, one cannot miss recognizing, at least in part, the layout of the forester's house in the Vorderriss. During the Christmas season, Thoma always declined invitations, preferring to spend Christmas Eve sitting in the solitude of his rustic living room, one wall of which bristled with hunting gear. There he would look at the lit Christmas tree and imagine himself sitting at the table with his father and mother in the forester's house in the Vorderriss.

II *School Years*

One year after the family had left the Vorderriss, on September 28, 1874, Thoma's father died in Forstenried. The change of climate had accelerated the decline of his health. Paralysis of the heart was given as the cause for his sudden death. Besides the unimaginable grief for mother and children, the loss meant the beginning of a continuous financial crisis. It was virtually impossible for the mother and her seven children to live on the one hundred marks she received as widow's pension. By a fortunate coincidence, a high of-ficial in the forest service took over the guardianship of the children. Some of her letters reflect the embarrassing situation Thoma's mother found herself in, begging for financial help time and again. This misery was aggravated by her own ailments from which she had suffered since the birth of her youngest daughter, Berta, in 1873. Repeatedly she had to spend several weeks with her sister in Oberammergau, to be under close medical attention. Following the advice of her doctor, she began to think about mov-ing to a warmer climate further away from Munich. She finally decided on the small village of Prien on the Chiemsee, where she rented and managed the hotel Zur Kampenwand in order to supple-ment her income.

In the meantime, Ludwig had reached school age. Entirely depending on scholarships, he finished his preschool years and one year of the *Lateinschule* at Landstuhl in the Palatinate. In 1876, he transferred to the seminary at Neuburg on the Danube, then to the *Lateinschule* at Burghausen on the Salzach. The most formative years of his pre-university education he spent at the Wilhelmsgym-nasium in Munich. When he finished the *Gymnasium* by passing the *Abitur* (the final examination) in Landshut, he had attended school at no less than five different places. His mother had spent countless hours worrying that her unruly son would drop out of school abruptly. Thoma himself makes a short but revealing remark concerning his turbulent high-school years in his "Autobiographische Skizze": "For a lively young fellow who had grown up in the woods, the pressures of school could not be a pleasure. And by no means did I ever extend any love to my teachers; first, to me they were mischief-makers, and later their dry natures repelled me."[3] Nothing could summarize his feelings vis-à-vis his tutors better than these two brief sentences. He was especially annoyed by their constant attempts to keep distance between themselves and their pupils, by which means they inevitably lost contact with their audience and turned into cranks and tyrants who suspected revolution everywhere they looked; or they became very detached individuals who did their duty groaningly, showing indifference or even hostility toward the students.[4] To respect the authority of the teachers was considered of utmost importance, and yet the teachers did not seem to realize how sensitive youth is to falsehood and exaggeration. Thoma soon began to believe that the best education is the one which inspires the youngster with an aversion to tactlessness and immodesty. Another precondition for any reasonable education he saw in a cordial relationship between pupil and teacher. The severe restrictions which school imposed on its students led even the most decent among Thoma's comrades to violations of these laws, just to show their bravery. Thoma had good reasons for registering massive complaints against the schools he attended. One incident which almost made him commit suicide recalled, for him, all the inhumane aspects of this environment. It had to do with a silly little love letter addressed to a young girl Thoma had admired for quite a while. By coincidence, his teacher found the letter in one of his school books during class and handed it over to the headmaster, who immediately took the opportunity to warn a reputable family in town that Ludwig, who had frequently been a guest in their house, had intended to address the improper letter to the youngest daughter of the house. Ludwig was not only outraged by the atrocity of this action, but even more so by the fact that his headmaster had not told the truth about the letter. Ludwig's attempts to explain the matter to the family were in vain. The only person on the faculty who did not take part in the harassment campaign against him which followed the incident was the chaplain. His gentle understanding kept the young Thoma from total desperation. Among his colleagues, Ludwig did not find one who showed compassion for him. They all acted like narrow-minded little Philistines, caring only for their own interests.[5]

Thoma expressed very warm feelings for the humanistically oriented education in general, because it involved the student at an early age in the study of the classical languages and literatures. Through the beauty of the classical languages, he learned about the immutability of natural feeling *per se*. Mathematics, on the other hand, was not one of Thoma's favorite subjects, mainly because it demands "continuous progress from the student and does not encourage dash."[6] His declared favorite was history, a subject in which he refused to follow the school curriculum to the letter; instead, he indulged in reading the great standard works of his time. Sometimes he involved himself so deeply in these materials that on the way to school he held fiery speeches against Anjou or Rome. As far as the teachers at the Munich *Gymnasium* were concerned, history extended only to the year 1815. The subsequent events seemed too topical and, hence, too dangerous to be treated in class. Problems of a similar nature arose for Thoma's literature teachers, mainly because not all literary works are morally fit for education. Since warning the students of delicate passages would draw attention to them, the teachers acted as if they took the students' shy disgust for granted, which, in turn, produced a humorous reaction from the class.

At this point already, Thoma's interest in German literature could not be satisfied by regular class assignments. He and one of his comrades began attending the lectures of the famous Professor Bernays at the University of Munich. Thoma's personal library had already reached a respectable size, but the acquisitions mainly consisted of cheaply bound volumes. His mother, who had to pay for the books, was not entirely happy with her son's proclivity, and she frequently let her feelings be known by shaking her head in despair.

And then there was the theater. Munich, already a cultural metropolis, offered many opportunities for the young stage fan. Although the theater was officially off limits to the pupils, Thoma spent many delightful hours in the balcony of the *Hoftheater*. The tickets were usually provided by his aunt, who also counted herself among the theater experts. Long before opening time, Thoma patiently waited in front of the theater, a piece of bread and a hunk of sausage in his pocket, in case he got hungry.

During his school years in Munich, Thoma lived in the household of two distant relatives, who had kindly offered him one room in their small apartment. "Uncle" Joseph, a retired official of the postal service, was the husband of "Uncle" Wilhelm's sister. Wilhelm was a former army lieutenant, liberal in his views but full of memories of his time in the service and of the battles of Wörth, Sedan, and Orleans. Joseph's view of modern times was a very pessimistic one. For him, the year 1866 marked the end of the good old days. He remained an old-style conservative and despised the distinctly anti-Catholic politics of the Bismarck administration after the foundation of the Second Empire in 1871. Bismarck's policy ultimately led to the so-called *Kulturkampf*, a clash between Bismarck and the Catholic Church in the *Reich*. Bismarck promoted the introduction of civil marriage and the suppression of the Jesuit order. After a battle of nearly sixteen years, he had to give in, and most of the new laws which were aimed against the autonomy of the Catholic Church in Gemany had to be suspended. In spite of their conflicting political views, the two "uncles" got along quite well. On hot summer evenings, "Uncle" Joseph, his wife, and Ludwig often went to one of Munich's numerous beer gardens.

Munich had not, by that time, become the metropolis it is today. All around the city's center were gardens, meadows, and even farms. From Ludwig's window the peaks of the northern Alps could be seen on clear days. Life in the city still had something soothing about it. A threat to this leisurely way of life was seen in the increasing Prussian influence after 1871, and the "Old Bavarians" took every opportunity to show their hostility against the intruders from the North. This old antagonism between North and South surfaces in many of Thoma's later works, in which he points out the humorous aspects of the eternal feud, rather than the serious ones.

Ludwig still enjoyed the tranquillity of old Munich, especially on Sundays when he accompanied "Uncle" Joseph on his walks through the city. The elderly gentleman had lived in the Bavarian capital all his life, and had seen many changes in its appearance, not all to his liking. Sometimes on their walks, the "uncle" was able to proudly point out to Ludwig one of Munich's celebrities, for instance the famous Paul Heyse, who already had the aura of a poet laureate.

It was not only in Munich that Ludwig had the opportunity to see famous personalities. At home in Prien on the Chiemsee, where he spent his vacations, in addition to enjoying his freedom from the routine of his studies and the beautiful outdoors, he helped in entertaining the guests in his mother's hotel. His favorite job was to ferry them to the *Herreninsel* in a rowboat. On this island, King Ludwig II had begun to build his dream castle, *Herrenchiemsee*, which was to be the Bavarian Versailles. The population, however, saw this huge new enterprise as a sign of the king's accelerating madness. Among Ludwig's passengers were men like Felix Dahn, who became famous through his novel *Der Kampf um Rom*. A very

choleric gentleman of short stature and temper was Friedrich
Theodor Vischer, a renowned poet and professor of esthetics at the
University of Tübingen.

One of the most memorable events during Ludwig's summers in
Prien was the brief appearance of Otto von Bismarck, who was passing through on a journey to Bad Gastein. Waiting among a crowd of
townspeople, Ludwig saw the Iron Chancellor at the train station.
Bismarck, standing at the window of his private railroad car, asked
the nervous town mayor, who was standing in front of the festively
dressed crowd, whether the town was Prien or not. In High German
pronunciation the word obviously seemed unfamiliar to the mayor
and he hastily answered: "No, Prean," pronouncing the name in
the local dialect, at which the crowd burst into laughter over the
poor man's *faux pas*. For Ludwig, who saw Bismarck as the personification of Germany's greatness, an old dream had come true,
especially since he had found Bismarck's physical appearance just as
impressive as he had always imagined it.

Ludwig's scholastic torture came to an end when he passed the
final examination in August 1886. At the festive beer party, a standard event following graduation, Ludwig had to hold the formal address. But in the middle of his second sentence, he froze, and the
headmaster had to save the occasion by jumping in with a well-set
speech to the students. Thoma never felt comfortable speaking in
public. He much preferred to collect his thoughts quietly and to put
them down on paper. The only occasion at which he later gave a
public speech was at the unveiling of the Perfall Monument in
Schliersee.

III   *University and Professional Years*

Ludwig Thoma's true love always belonged to the forest and its
inhabitants. It was only natural that he should decide during the
summer vacations of 1886 to study forestry at the academy in
Aschaffenburg. In his decision, he found solid support among the
members of his family. A particularly strong argument was to be
made for studying forestry since it seemed likely that a scholarship
could be obtained from sources within the forestry department for
the son of a former member of the royal forest service. It also seemed proper that Ludwig should continue the old family tradition of
serving in the king's forest service.

In the fall of 1886, Ludwig entered the foresters' academy.

Everything was to his liking at the beginning, especially the new freedom he enjoyed as a university student. Life in the student union, excursions into the Spessart forest, and social gatherings enthralled him, but the studies obviously failed to do so. In December 1886 he wrote to his new guardian, Oberforstrat Ludwig von Raesfeldt: "As far as the foresters' academy is concerned, everything goes its old way . . . as far as life in the Corps (student union) is concerned, one could not imagine it more beautiful. . . ."[7] But on August 9, 1887, he explained his lack of progress in school to Baron Raesfeldt:

Yes, it has to be said finally; it was a missed vocation. I always took great delight in the forest and in nature, but to investigate, to study it, never agreed with me. . . . Often I did not go to the lectures because I sat at home with an old book out of which I made excerpts; yes, as a candidate of forestry, I translated Horace instead of dealing with mathematics. . . . I have decided to study law. I think I may predict that I shall achieve something there. This, at least, I can promise you, . . . that I will go to work with determination and that I shall be industrious.[8]

For Thoma's mother and for "old Viktor," his decision meant great disappointment. It added more sadness to their already gloomy mood, caused by an incident of rent fraud which had occurred in the hotel shortly before. Signs of the mother's old ailment began to show again, making the future of her family seem increasingly uncertain. Nevertheless, Ludwig entered law school in Munich in the fall of 1887.

We know little of the following three semesters of study. It is apparent, however, that the student unions had finally lost their attraction for Ludwig: only a few months were spent with the Corps Suevia, after which he lived a relatively solitary life, enjoying the art scene of Munich, sharpening his eye and gaining a deeper understanding for painting and architecture. During his long strolls through the city and the suburbs he talked to people of all walks of life, visited churches and old houses, and walked about in Schwabing, the traditional home of bohemians and students near the university. He occasionally buried himself for hours in one of the art galleries, particularly in the Neue Pinakothek, or in the contemporary art exhibitions, where he tried to improve his understanding of art. He preferred to do things on his own rather than to depend on formal schooling.

At the beginning of the spring semester, 1889, we find Thoma as a student at Erlangen. We do not know why he changed universities. One factor leading to the decision might have been the rumor that examinations at Erlangen were easier than in Munich. It may also have been Thoma's concern that the distractions of the big city might affect his studies. Whatever it was that made him go to the small university nestled within a plain, insignificant little town north of Nuremberg, he certainly found the right climate for a speedy conclusion to his studies. The constant admonitions from Baron von Raesfeldt and his mother also helped him realize the necessity of working hard toward the degree. In the spring of 1890, he was able to report to his jubilant mother that he would try for an examination date in August. He stuck to this promise and passed the final examination with success. The rascal had finally grown up. When he left the examination room, some of his friends were waiting to beat his top hat down until it burst at his ears (an old custom at the University of Erlangen). The townsfolk, who were used to being involved in university matters and student customs, greeted the graduate with respect.

Thoma found little praise, however, for the way in which law studies were conducted at Erlangen. "Looking back at my studies, I can say that I mostly studied out of books and that I did not feel any of the (so-called) determining influence of the teacher."[9] But for some individual professors he found kind words: "They were rather old gentlemen, and they seemed to me like relics from the time of Uhland [Ludwig Uhland, a German poet of the Romantic period]; they also fit the picture of this small university town, where one can see so many plaques reminding one of famous theologians, physicians, and lawyers. They were cranks of the kind you can get homesick for."[10]

During the last semester of Thoma's studies in Erlangen Bismarck was dismissed. What particularly angered Thoma were not the triumphant outcries of the chancellor's enemies, but the lethargic and indifferent way in which the Germans reacted to this arbitrary action of the young emperor. A cartoon in an English newspaper, showing the pilot (Bismarck) disembarking from the German ship, caught Thoma's attention. But no similar signs of disapproval appeared in German newspapers. Most people seemed to have forgotten Bismarck's merits.[11]

After a short vacation during which Thoma recovered from the strains of the examination, professional life finally began for him. In dress coat and top hat he walked down the street one morning to take his oath of office, thereby entering public service as an assistant attorney. He started his work with utmost dedication and the highest ethical standards. Very soon, however, he began to see the inherent flaws of bureaucracy and the cynical attitudes of some of his colleagues. His boss, who headed the district court, soon showed himself to be a petty character who took pleasure in dealing with the smallest misdemeanors, elaborating, for example, on what might have been the "criminal intentions of a tramp who had found a horseshoe and who had not turned it in to the authorities."[12] This man, with his rude way of dealing, and his suspiciousness and complacency, certainly did little to win Thoma's respect for the law profession, much less to awaken the young man's desire to commit himself to a career as an official in the court system. Not only his superiors managed to dampen Thoma's enthusiasm, but also his clients. Occasionally Thoma was detached by the court to the duty of a counsel for the defense. Initially, he took his task very seriously. He conferred with the prisoners at length and composed a well-set speech, stressing sentiment and compassion. When he delivered it before the court, he had to discover to his great disappointment that virtually nobody was listening to him, neither the judges nor the clients. Even his expectation of a word of thanks or a hearty handshake offered by the client, turned out to be in vain. Not much more inspiring was the way Thoma saw his colleagues carry on their duties.

What a disappointment bureaucracy was for the young lawyer! How much Thoma detested the arrogance of his colleagues, for whom relaxation meant a walk to the railroad station in the company of other equally pedantic comrades *in iure* discussing recent cases, formulating stilted sentences, or gossiping about the incompetence and senility of one of their fellow bureaucrats. For them, the main attraction in town, Dürrenmatt-style, was the arrival of the evening express Paris-Vienna, which stopped for half a minute: "One looked contemptuously at the strange people who had no idea about introductory and concluding sentences, and the strangers looked contemptuously at the ulsters and worn-out shoes of the scribes. One repelled the other until the train departed. The strangers went to Vienna, the counsels toward a beer hall where fresh thoughts about new court rulings flashed through their minds."[13]

In December 1890 we find Thoma briefly in Erlangen again,

where he finished his studies by acquiring the Doctor of Laws
degree. Although his studies had been officially completed by the
"state examination," the degree meant added prestige. Disgusted
by the pedantry and staleness of civil service and of the court in particular, he began thinking about opening up his own law office in
Traunstein, which would enable him, uninhibited by service
regulations, to contribute articles to a newspaper or to write essays
on the side. In addition, he would find time to hunt and enjoy a
more leisurely life in this lovely small town. In spite of his displeasure with the district court, he did not feel uncomfortable in the
social climate of Traunstein, which was dominated by a prosperous,
benevolent middle class whose live-and-let-live attitude suited him
well. But things were to turn out differently: Professor Hecht from
Vienna, a summer guest in his mother's inn, predicted that Thoma
would not want to spend his life as a small-town lawyer in Traunstein, but would one day go to Munich, where he would win fame
as a writer and journalist. Although Thoma liked hearing such
things, he wrote them off as daydreams. First of all, where should
he obtain the funds essential for starting a career in a metropolis
like Munich? A solution to this problem presented itself very soon,
however, when another guest, whom Thoma calls Assessor F.,
offered the necessary funds.

Yet another factor contributed to the final decision to leave
Traunstein for Munich. Two of Ludwig's brothers, Max and Peter,
had emigrated to Australia eight years earlier. Now, in a letter,
Peter announced his return to Bavaria. His mother immediately
gave up the inn she had managed in Traunstein and acquired
another hotel in Seebruck on the Chiemsee. There were many
repairs to be made in the house, and the aging mother saw this as a
way of keeping her son Peter at home. The plan unfortunately did
not materialize.

Thoma's move to Munich finally came in February 1893. He was
fully aware of the significance of the change: "I do not think that
any event has had such a decisive influence on my life as has the
move to Munich; there I found connections to men who encouraged
me to start as a writer, and, most of all, I myself found the courage
to do so. I also lost the taste for covering myself with the blanket of
a comfortable Philistine's life."[14] The big world, which he could
now appreciate much more than in his *Gymnasium* days, unfolded
itself before his eyes. During the first few months, the new job commanded his attention. For eight weeks he worked for the Munich

city administration, then he entered the large and famous law firm of Löwenfeld as an assistant attorney. Initially impressed by the hectic pace in the city courts, he soon found out that some of its important-looking employees were human beings with considerable shortcomings. This did not prevent him, however, from admiring some of the outstanding champions of the court. One of them, Bernstein, an associate of his boss, Löwenfeld, was for Thoma the personification of a successful lawyer, writer, and celebrated critic — in other words, a man who had accomplished everything Thoma himself wanted to become.

There was no shortage of new friends. In the old Nürnberger Wurstküche zum Herz (called "Herzl" by the natives), where Thoma ate lunch every day, he soon belonged to a circle of permanent guests who formed a *Stammtisch*. Among the *Stammtisch* members was Joseph Ritter, the editor of the *Augsburger Abendzeitung*, a man who later influenced Thoma's life significantly. Ritter liked the way Thoma carried himself in the lively discussions which went on every noon at the "Herzl," and one day he suggested that he put some of his thoughts on paper, since they might be suitable for publication in his paper. Quickly Thoma produced a few essays on current problems and, to his great pleasure, found them printed in the *Abendzeitung*. Since the associate editors of the paper were also fond of Thoma's style, he was encouraged to continue his contributions. Thoma's career as a journalist had begun.

These essays were not the only products of his newly awakened ambitions as a writer, however. There were also poems, most of which were written in coarse, Middle Bavarian dialect, some in a serious mood, and others with humorous undertones. They quickly became popular with his friends.

The literary scene in Germany was very lively at that time. Gerhart Hauptmann had just published his first naturalistic dramas, provoking one theater scandal after the other in Berlin. *Vor Sonnenaufgang*, the first of Hauptmann's works which Thoma read, made a lasting impression on the young writer. On the other hand, he did not think very highly of Sudermann's *Die Ehre* because some of its characters and their stilted language reminded him of the shallow literary entertainment which Eugenie Marlitt's popular novels provided.

Already at this early stage, Thoma began to take a liking to Theodor Fontane, whose novel *Frau Jenny Treibel* first drew his attention. In Fontane's slightly detached but benevolently humorous manner of describing the world around him, Thoma saw the realization of one of Goethe's demands, namely that the writer's personality should manifest itself in his work. And what a likeable personality Fontane was for Thoma! He remained one of Thoma's favorite writers even in his later years. Achieving his particular kind of realism, not imposing but showing life as it is, seemed to be the true task for a good writer, and it was undoubtedly to be preferred to the mere description of moods and feelings. Fontane's delicate verbal paintings of an epoch convey distinctly greater and more lasting impressions to future generations than the books of a historian. In Thoma's opinion, civilization and its changes could be captured best in the literary medium.

At the *Stammtisch*, the different "isms" in contemporary literature, particularly Naturalism and Realism, as well as the dying Idealism of the nineteenth century, were fervently discussed. The more conservative members of Thoma's "round table" deplored the desire of these new movements to bring ugliness and dirt into art. The discussions were by no means limited to literary subjects. Art in general, particularly painting, was of great interest to the participants, especially since painters also belonged to the group. Their concern was the increasing influence of Impressionism. Not always to the liking of his friends, Thoma vigorously defended the new movements and their spirit, sometimes by throwing himself into fiery verbal battles. Since most of the members of the "round table" were "Old Bavarians," hearty expressions occasionally spiced the disputations.

In December 1893 Thoma had to take the Bavarian state bar examination, known as the much-feared *Staatskonkurs*. It was an unwritten law that anybody who passed this examination with at least the grade of "2" ("B") would have no difficulty obtaining a civil-service position. But one who received a "3" ("C") would be treated more or less like a misfit. Not even the post-office department or the railroads would be interested in his services. Thoma passed the examination, but he does not tell us what grade he received. Considering his apathetic attitude toward the law profession, it may well have been a "3." Nevertheless, for several weeks preceding the examination, he involved himself with "a certain passion" in legal questions, "for the first, but also for the last time."[15] He had fulfilled all the requirements his profession demanded, and, relieved of a burden, he left Munich to spend some time on the Chiemsee, at his mother's inn at Seebruck.

The homecoming was not a happy one. Thoma found his mother to be in rapidly declining health. It depressed him terribly that he had not yet been able to show her any concrete success as a lawyer or as a writer, which would have rewarded her for endless years of concern and hope. During her last days some of his articles appeared in the *Augsburger Abendzeitung*. As Thoma read them to her, she put her frail hand into his, seeming to want to assure him that she believed that everything would turn out all right for him. He decided to stay in Seebruck, awaiting the bitter end. In June she died, leaving him without a home.

Shortly after the funeral, Thoma returned to Munich, still full of doubts about his future. For a short while he held the position of an assistant in a law firm. To open his own law office in the city was out of the question since he completely lacked the capital necessary for a successful start. The old plan to start a career in Traunstein was also discarded. But it was impossible to stay in his old job. It barely paid for his living expenses. He had to make a move, but he did not know which one.

Once again, Thoma's future was decided by coincidence. He had taken a train to Dachau, a small town approximately twenty kilometers from Munich, to hike from there to nearby Schwabenhausen. The rich agricultural area around Dachau immediately fascinated him: "As we came up the hill, and the town square with its gabled houses lay in front of me in true peace, a great desire to live here in this tranquillity overcame me."[16] Although practically all of his friends advised against a move to Dachau, he made the decision. Two months later he moved into the house of a Dachau tailor. He had about one hundred marks in his pocket, and prided himself on being the first practicing lawyer in town.

At first, Thoma must have looked like an exotic animal to the townspeople of Dachau, but after a rather cool reception they soon got used to his presence. His first prospective client, a portly farmer who came to Thoma's office on market day, gave him some introduction to the mentality of the country people. As the farmer began to explain his case, and Thoma started to make some notes, as every lawyer would do, the old man quickly put his hand on Thoma's arm and said: "No, don't write, don't write." As far as the good man was concerned, matters became serious only when something was put down on paper. After this incident, a few days went by during which no visitors showed up. Thoma's anxiety began to grow until it reached the stage of desperation before the tide suddenly began to turn. A schoolteacher, who was being sued for libel by the mayor of his town and by the district supervisor, sought his counsel. The teacher had been referred by a traveling salesman who sold a number of books to the young lawyer. Before long, business began to pick up and Thoma's budget soon allowed him to invite "old Viktor" to join him and keep his household, a call to which the faithful old soul responded more than enthusiastically. Her little protégé, whom she had carried in her arms some twenty-five years earlier, was now *Herr Doktor*. In addition to her household chores, Viktor willingly undertook some of the clerical work in the office. She soon became known to Ludwig's clients as *Frau Mutter*. They welcomed the personal interest she took in their problems, and often talked to her about their cases in the kitchen if Thoma happened to be out of the office. In this way, she became an important mediator between the *Herr Doktor* and the simple coun-tryfolk, who already felt understood and comforted after these talks with Viktor.

It was a quiet time for Thoma, who found ample leisure to read and to study the population of the countryside surrounding Dachau. It is an appealing landscape of rolling hills with open spaces speck-led with small clusters of woods and scenic villages. The people of this region were as appealing to Thoma as was the countryside. Rugged farmers, they were equipped with a strong sense of right and wrong. He began to recognize that their undistorted view of life originated in their work, which totally fulfilled their lives. Com-pared to their genuine concept of duty and honor, Thoma found the moral code of the so-called intellectuals hollow and artificial. Honesty was also reflected in the vocabulary of the farmer's ex-pressive dialect, a concrete language which called things by their true names. It was certainly not a very delicate speech, but it suited these plain-speaking people, to whom even disease and death were natural occurrences, and for whom there was little room for daydreaming and sensitivity. Their unspoiled and honest way of life stood in sharp contrast to that which Thoma had witnessed during his time at the courts of Traunstein and Munich.

One day while riding the train to Munich, Thoma had the idea to write about these farmers he was slowly beginning to understand. Shortly afterwards, a series of short stories depicting episodes out of the lives of the countryfolk began to appear in the *Sammler* (an in-sert of the *Augsburger Abendzeitung*). In 1897, these stories were collected in a book Thoma called *Agricola*. The first critical review of the stories was given by the group, later known as *Stellwagen* (coach), whose members held meetings every evening in the Zieglerbräu, a well-known tavern. The small group consisted mainly of town officials who claimed thorough knowledge of the country-folk around Dachau. Especially the gentlemen from the county courthouse were skeptical about the rather favorable treatment the farmers had received in Thoma's book. In their eyes, the farmers were stubborn, unruly people who would do anything to make life as difficult as possible for a royal Bavarian civil servant. The county supervisor who took part in the sessions of the *Stellwagen* was a born dictator, and he loved nothing better than bureaucracy. The district attorney hated the rural environment and longed for the city and its "cultivated" people. The only official among the group who demonstrated any human understanding for the farmers was "a member of a dying race," as Thoma describes him, "[of] arch-Bavarian district judges of the old order." This old district judge was held in high esteem by the farmers, who even endured his occasional rudeness because they knew that he had a good heart and that, deep in his soul, he liked them.

Thoma came to rural Bavaria at a time when the overwhelming influence the clergy had once exerted on the population was rapidly declining. Before the so-called Caprivi Treaties, designed by the German Chancellor Georg Leo Graf von Caprivi to liberalize trade by lowering customs barriers, went into effect, the farmers had voted their parish priests to the assembly in Munich almost as a rule since they themselves had been totally disinterested in politics. Now, since grain prices were subject to dumping, both the political abstention and the legendary support for the clergy nearly disappeared. After 1893, the farmers banded together in the *Bauernbund* (farmer's union) and nominated their own candidates for the elections.

Although Dachau was still a small "backwoods" town in the 1890's, it by no means was lacking in culture. A colony of well-known painters had its domicile there. The most famous painter of the "Dachau school," Adolf Hölzel (1853-1934), had found an ideal environment in this tranquil town with its picturesque houses and its undisturbed character. Through Hölzel, who was a pleasant fellow of Austrian origin, Thoma got to know some of the new writers to whom he had so far paid little attention. One of these was Tolstoy, whose *Anna Karenina* later became one of Thoma's favorite literary works. Henrik Ibsen was also among this group. His

Baumeister Solness did not impress Thoma as much as it should have according to its reputation, because its action was contrived and the characters seemed rather stilted for Thoma's taste. Already at this point in his career, one can detect a strong sense of independence in Thoma's literary judgment; it would very soon grow into a distinctly nonconformist attitude. As Thoma notes, his defiance of Ibsen and his fame almost branded him as a heretic in the light of the Norwegian's theatrical triumphs in Berlin. In retrospect, Thoma gives us a recipe for gaining independence in judging literature: one should watch for the hidden secrets of composition and style because they are the only place in which one can observe the author in the creative process. One should learn to guess the author's mood from his words, and his thought from the mood. In his opinion, this manner of literary appreciation could best be learned from Gottfried Keller. [17]

In the meantime, business had picked up, allowing Thoma a moderate but comfortable lifestyle. Dachau really began to grow on him. In his *Erinnerungen,* Thoma does not elaborate much on these happy times, but in one of his sketches, entitled "Wilhelm Diez," in the collection *Leute, die ich kannte* (People I Knew), he captures some of the atmosphere of *Gemütlichkeit* which he enjoyed in Dachau. [18] These quiet times were a sort of intermezzo, a period of presentiment and preparation for the final step into the literary world, which was to come sooner than Thoma thought. On the first of January, 1896, the journal *Jugend* (Youth) was founded by Georg Hirth in Munich. Its second issue contained a political poem by Thoma who had hesitantly submitted his contribution shortly after having seen the first issue of the periodical, whose primary task was to bring new life into the artistic scene in Germany, mainly young writers. Thoma's first contribution to the new journal was followed by several others, and his confidence in his own talent began to grow.

While Thoma was still in Dachau, the hotel in Seebruck, which was owned by the Thoma children after his mother died, was finally sold, and his older sister moved to Munich, where she bought a boardinghouse to run as a *pension* for tourists. The plan of Ludwig's coming to join her and to open a law office in Munich was discussed. Once while visiting the *pension* Thoma was asked by a guest if he was the author of some poems which had appeared in *Jugend.* The gentleman, who turned out to be Eduard Graf von Keyserling, author of several well-known novels, then urged Thoma not to stay out of the mainstream of new ideas, but to involve himself fully in the emerging literary movement. This would of course have meant giving up the tranquillity of Dachau and moving to Munich again. While this was part of Thoma's long-range plans, he was a bit reluctant to abandon his newly established law practice in the country. He also felt bound by a commitment he had undertaken with an old friend and former fellow student to jointly open a law firm in Munich, an enterprise which would demand some time of preparation. Furthermore, he was just not eager to leave his cozy corner in Dachau. It was, after all, the first place after the Vorderriss where he had grown some roots.

On a spring day in 1896, Ritter, the editor of the *Augsburger Abendzeitung*, came storming into Thoma's Dachau office. He was flashing a copy of a new pictorial magazine, loudly advocating that one should not be quiet in the face of such happenings and that everything short of police action and censorship should be used against such a publication. He urged Thoma to immediately write a bristling article expressing formal disapproval of the new journal. The illustrated magazine to which Ritter so violently objected was the first issue of *Simplicissimus*, a highly controversial, satirical magazine whose editor Thoma would become in later years.

Approximately a year after Thoma's initial acquaintance with the *Simplicissimus*, the planned move to Munich materialized. The early days in Munich were marked by a rather sad event, the death of his sister. "Old Viktor," who had reluctantly left Dachau with Thoma, seemed neither able nor willing to adapt to the new environment and could never understand why her protégé had left such comfortable circumstances in Dachau.

Contributing to the melancholic mood of these first months in Munich were Thoma's experiences at the office. Most depressing was the realization that the recipe for success as a court lawyer seemed to require that he conduct himself as a people's tribune, a sentimental actor who must capture the audience with statements full of pathos even when talking about legal technicalities. Thoma was much too straightforward and professional in his approach to interpreting the law for this kind of stage-acting, and soon became convinced that the legal profession was not suited to him after all.

The disheartening mood of these early days in Munich soon gave way to a fresh optimism when Thoma learned that his peasant stories had been accepted for publication, in the form of a book, to come out under the aegis of Waldbauer's bookstore in Passau. He

immediately wrote to Bruno Paul, the illustrator of the
Simplicissimus, who, after a meeting with Thoma, agreed to furnish
illustrations for the book. But the matter was not as simple as
Thoma had expected. Paul was overloaded with work for the
Simplicissimus, and it was not until the late summer of 1897 that he
was able to work on his drawings for Thoma's book, which were
finally completed in October. Now that the book was ready to be
compiled, Thoma, Bruno Paul, and Rudolf Wilke, another member
of the *Simplicissimus* staff, who later became one of Thoma's close
friends, worked on one Sunday afternoon to put text and pictures
together in the right order. Two months later, in December, the
book was published under the appropriate title *Agricola*. So proud
was Thoma to see his first book prominently displayed in the window of Munich's renowned bookstore, Littauer, that he spent the
next few days taking extensive walks through the city to check the
display cases of other bookstores. His friends from the *Stammtisch*
at the "Herzl" who had helped him in completing his first major
publication were invited to his home for a lavish venison dinner in
genuine old-Bavarian style. Peculiarly enough, the most favorable
reviews came from the North of Germany. But in Munich the book
was also praised as an excellent portrait of rural Bavarian life.
Thoma could finally regard himself as a writer; an old dream had
now become reality.

Probably the most significant benefit of the work on *Agricola*
were the new contacts with the editorial staff of the *Simplicissimus*.
The attention of Albert Langen, the *Simplicissimus* boss, had been
alerted, and he quickly invited the young writer to visit him. The
first meeting of the two men who later worked together so closely
did not end on the most cordial terms. Thoma, the straightforward
Bavarian who thoroughly disliked formalities, found Langen a nervous individual who jumped from one question to another, trying to
keep the initiative at all times during the conversation. Moreover,
Thoma seemed to detect in Langen's conversation a slight pity for
him as a South German. It was enough to make his responses appear
harsher and shorter than usual. In later years, when the two had
become close friends, they often talked about their first meeting,
which had ended in discord.

Something else had contributed to Thoma's initial skepticism toward Langen: according to rumors, Langen was a pampered tycoon
whose interest in the publishing business was strictly financial. The
truth was that Langen had founded his small publishing house with

the remainder of his father's estate, which consisted of a rather modest sum. However, since he was thought to be a wealthy man, his caution vis-à-vis some of the more generous plans made by his staff was interpreted as stinginess.

Another obstacle in the way of an immediate understanding between Thoma and Langen was their completely different backgrounds. In contrast to Thoma's modest bourgeois home, Langen had grown up in lavish surroundings. His father was a very successful businessman in Cologne, where he owned a large sugar plant. The invention of the sugar cube had made him a rich man. When he died, he left an estate of one million marks to each of his children. There were several stories in circulation about how the young Langen had lost most of his inheritance. One version was that he went to Paris to start a brandy factory. Another one professed that he wanted to become either a painter or a poet in Montmartre. Whatever it was he intended to do in Paris, that is where his wealth had shrunk to almost nothing. At the Montmartre, Langen met the Danish painter (and swindler) Willy Gretor, a limping, red-haired man who persuaded the young Langen to buy a series of old paintings. Already an art connoisseur, Langen was fascinated by the idea of possessing a gallery of old masters. Shortly after the purchase, he discovered that only a few of the "master works" were originals; the rest consisted of cheap copies. Outraged by the fraud, Langen put all the blame on Gretor, who seemed unbothered by the reproaches. For Gretor wealth was immoral in the first place, and loosing it this way was just punishment for a green young fellow. But, as a quasireparation for the loss he had indirectly caused Langen, he promised to introduce him to influential Scandinavian friends, especially to the poet Björnstjerne Björnson. He also offered to use his connections to figures in contemporary French literary life in order to help the young adventurer. As an additional compensation, he was also ready to present a splendid idea of his own, which, if realized, would make Langen a wealthy man again.

Gretor's plan called for the creation of a German counterpart to the extremely popular and successful French satiric publication *Gil Blas*. As almost always in Langen's life, plans turned into reality faster than could have been anticipated. He was introduced to Björnson, who in turn introduced him to the stars of Scandinavian literature, e.g., August Strindberg and Knut Hamsun. Langen fell in love with Björnson's daughter, Dagny, who could do nothing but laugh about the nervous, short German fellow, at first, but who nevertheless became his wife shortly thereafter. After a string of disappointments, Langen felt his old enthusiasm coming back. It was at this point that he decided to start his own publishing company, which would enable him to make his beloved Scandinavian writers popular in Germany. Mentioning his personal acquaintances among the Scandinavian and French writers in a circular letter to all German booksellers—Marcel Proust was indeed personally known to him—Langen convinced enough of them to place orders, to make his new enterprise successful. Some of the translations of French and Scandinavian novels soon reached an edition of more than a hundred thousand copies. Another of Gretor's ingenious hints led Langen to new ideas: the cartoonist Thomas Theodor Heine was hired and put in charge of the cover designs. This very gifted artist made it possible to start the German *Gil Blas*. Printing an initial edition of four hundred thousand copies, which turned out to be much too many, he started his pictorial journal under the title *Simplicissimus*, which was suggested by Heine, who afterwards expressed fear that its awkwardness might prevent it from catching on with the German public. But it was impossible to restrain Langen once he had become convinced of the idea. The first issue turned out to be hardly a cut above the level of the common *Gartenlaube*, as far as quality was concerned. But Langen's legendary stubbornness soon began to pay off.

In spite of their initial misunderstandings, Thoma concluded an agreement with Langen to help in building an image for the new publication. Rudolf Wilke, Eduard Thöny, Korfiz Holm, and Ferdinand von Reznicek, Thoma's co-workers in the editor's office, were congenial colleagues, all determined to turn the *Simplicissimus*, as the magazine was already commonly called, into Germany's satirical eye. There was also Bruno Paul, an expert in drawing coarse Bavarian peasants.

It did not take long for Thoma to feel at home among the people of the *Simplicissimus*. Their favorite meeting place during the evenings was the Café Heck at the Odeonsplatz. A spontaneous understanding developed between Thoma and Wilke, the humorist from Braunschweig. One reason must have been Wilke's aversion to pose and pompousness. He possessed a rare combination of a jolly, carefree nature and the ability and dedication of a true artist. Coming from an affluent home—his father was an architect—he preferred to study art in Munich rather than to enter his father's firm. After he had produced a number of humoristic drawings for several Munich newspapers, he suddenly became famous when he won the first artist's competition of *Jugend*, for which he had submitted a motif which completely contradicted the jury's instructions. The picture was drawn on the last day before the contest deadline, and it turned out to be so perfect that the board declared Wilke the winner, contrary to its initial intentions. From that point on, Wilke became a regular contributor to *Jugend* and later to the *Simplicissimus.*

For Thoma, who still felt he could not fully rely on his own artistic judgment, Wilke became a guide and leader during Thoma's first few months at the *Simplicissimus.* He was the personification of a perfect artist, as far as Thoma was concerned, a modest but determined man who had every right to make fun of the artistic parvenus who populated Munich in large numbers. In the Torggelstube, the traditional meeting place of young artists, many of whom had inflated opinions of themselves, Wilke enjoyed sitting among these "immortals" to ask them questions in an intentionally humble manner, encouraging their eagerness to give him advice. Then he would quietly laugh about the dandies, never letting them know that he regarded them as fools.

As favorably as the new literary boom around the turn of the century affected the cultural life in Munich, it also produced many false blossoms. The new "genius cult" attracted not only genuine talents, but also some loudmouthed, incompetent swindlers, particularly in the literary field. In spite of all its trivial side effects, however, the new wave of artistic consciousness brought life into the stagnating literary scene.

Since more and more writers developed a social and political awareness, the time was not free of literary scandals. One of the most spectacular among the ensuing uproars was the one resulting from Frank Wedekind's satirical poem about Emperor Wilhelm II's visit to Palestine in 1898. It appeared in October of that year in the *Simplicissimus* accompanied by a cartoon showing Gottfried von Bouillon, the leader of the first crusade, and Emperor Friedrich Barbarossa holding the notorious "sun helmet" which Wilhelm II preferred to wear at special occasions. To top it all off, the following text accompanied the picture: "Don't laugh so dirty, Barbarossa! Our crusades really did not serve any purpose, either!" Just as the poem was going to print, Korfiz Holm, the editor-in-chief, showed it to Thoma and several other artists associated with the

Simplicissimus. Although Thoma found Th. Th. Heine's cartoon
and Wedekind's text very humorous, he urged Holm to withhold
them from publication. But it was too late to stop the presses. Holm
explained that the matter had been reviewed by a renowned lawyer
who saw no danger of possible government sanctions against the
Simplicissimus, and despite Thoma's insistence that it be
withdrawn, he gave the order for the printing to go ahead. Cartoon
and poem appeared in issue number thirty-one of the magazine and
provoked immediate reaction from the authorities. Legal action was
brought against all responsible staff members of the *Simplicissimus.*
Heine, the cartoonist, was summoned to Leipzig, where he was
detained pending investigation and later sentenced to six months in
jail. Langen fled to Switzerland, where Wedekind joined him in
Zürich. Wedekind later put the blame for the whole affair on
Langen, who, he claimed, had forced him to write the ill-famed
poem, exploiting his desolate financial situation. According to
Thoma, this charge was completely unfounded since Langen had
already demanded modification of the original version of the poem
which had been even more insulting than the final one.

For several weeks the *Simplicissimus* was publicly accused by its
opponents all over Germany of premeditated *lèse majesté* and of
economic speculation. Thoma retrospectively justified the
Simplicissimus's satiric account of Wilhelm II's Palestine trip by
pointing out the ridiculously pompous manner in which the German monarch had behaved during the event depicted in the poem.
A ruler, he argues, who continuously dwells on trivial matters, as
Wilhelm II did, ought not to be surprised when his personal conduct provokes criticism and even controversy.[19] In Thoma's opinion,
the request for moderation in the emperor's public statements made
by the German Parliament in 1908 should have been made ten years
earlier. It would have prevented many misunderstandings inside
and outside Germany. Wilhelm II's unwise and often insulting
public comments indeed helped in creating a rather unfavorable
image of the German *Reich.*

Particularly annoying to Thoma was the way in which the investigation of the "Heine case" was carried out. The examining
magistrate from Saxonia, who had been put in charge of the matter,
suspected that there was more material against the defendants to be
found in the editor's office of the *Simplicissimus* in Munich. Entirely disregarding the law, he applied for a search warrant and indeed
found a letter in the editor's rooms which was later used against Th.

Th. Heine. This flagrant violation of the law by an official of the judicial system, committed in order to avenge the publication of a cartoon and a funny poem, outraged the artists of the *Simplicissimus*. But it did not produce the same reaction from the public. The scandal nevertheless had its positive side as far as the *Simplicissimus* was concerned, since circulation climbed from 55,000 to 85,000 copies as a consequence. It was also most peculiar that the *Simplicissimus* had become more popular in the parts of Germany known to be arch-conservative—southern Bavaria, for instance—than it was in the traditionally liberal cities of the middle and northern regions. In spite of the still limited attention which the satirical monthly was receiving in the cultural centers of Germany, the *Simplicissimus* had already established itself as the alert guardian against the actions of an overpowering bureaucracy and its parochial views.

The vacuum created by the sudden departure of Langen, Heine, and Wedekind had to be filled somehow in order to guarantee the continued existence of the periodical. Nothing seemed more natural than Thoma's closer association with the editorial staff. He was already known to its members as a brilliant satirist and as a competent lawyer. After all, he had predicted the outcome of the "Palestine affair." Under the pseudonym "Peter Schlemihl," he began to contribute poems and short articles on a regular basis. With his increased participation in the editorial work of the *Simplicissimus*, his dissatisfaction with his law-office work began to grow. He was well aware, however, that it would be foolhardy to sacrifice his established existence by embarking on an uncertain career as a writer.

During spring and summer of 1899, Thoma worked vigorously on his new play, which he called *Witwen* (Widows). After finishing it, he cheerfully presented it to the stage director Savits, an old friend from Seebruck, expecting its immediate acceptance for the stage. But after reading it, Savits told him point-blank: "This egg has no yolk."[20] He assured Thoma that there were good scenes in the play, but that there would not be enough substance for a successful production. For a few days Thoma secluded himself in bitter resignation. He felt misunderstood by the world around him. But the depression did not last long. In going over the play again and again, he soon realized that the old stage pro had been right. He began to see that the milieu of peasants, of the law office, and of smalltown life in which he had moved for a considerable time had overwhelmed him nostalgically while he was writing the play. The result was a comedy based on the old motif of mistaken identity which had been drowned in its own local color. Although the play had been ill received, it had shown one important thing to Thoma: his future as a writer would lie in portraying the world of the Bavarian farmer, which had long since become part of his life without his having realized it. One more thing was now settled in his mind: he would have to find a buyer for his law business. A solution offered itself before long: in September 1899 a lawyer friend asked him if he would consider selling his practice. He did not immediately accept the offer, although he welcomed it secretly with enthusiasm. Instead, he talked the matter over with his assistant, who urged him not to sell the practice to his friend, because he wanted to take it over himself under the same conditions. Thoma readily agreed and the next day the deal was concluded. To make his newly won freedom complete, Thoma rented a small house in Allershausen, a quaint village near Freising, in order to provide a home for "old Viktor" and one of his unmarried sisters. Viktor had been quite unhappy in the city and was yearning to get back to the countryside. The solution was beneficial to everyone, and Ludwig promised to visit the two ladies as often as time would permit. He moved into an unfurnished apartment on Munich's Lerchenfeldstrasse, feeling "free as a bird."[21]

Thoma was now a permanent staff member of the *Simplicissimus* and as such he received a regular salary of three thousand marks annually. The only stipulation in his contract was that he make one contribution a week. Initially, this was usually done in the form of a satirical poem depicting a current political event. Soon it became apparent that Thoma and Th. Th. Heine had become the spiritual leaders of the *Simplicissimus*, although the two did not always agree on everything. Heine, not very well liked by the rest of the staff because of his difficult personality, earned Thoma's respect with his biting sarcasm and his hard-hitting cartoons. He created the famous red bulldog character which served as a symbol for the *Simplicissimus's* defiance of suppression and narrow-mindedness. Wilhelm Schulz sent his cartoons from Berlin, and I. B. Engel occasionally submitted some of his drawings. Thoma enjoyed fairly close contact with the literary contributors Otto Julius Bierbaum, Arthur Holitscher, Leo Greiner-Falkenberg, and Hans von Gumppenberg, all of whom came into the editor's office from time to time. There was also a serious young man who served as a reader and occasionally wrote articles for the *Simplicissimus*. This slim young fellow was Thomas Mann, who used to come into Thoma's office dressed in the uniform of a Bavarian infantryman, since he was serving as an *Einjähriger* at that time. Everyone at the *Simplicissimus* knew that he was in the process of writing a novel which later appeared under the title *Buddenbrooks*.

Soon after Thoma had joined the *Simplicissimus* staff, he met Björnstjerne Björnson, Langen's father-in-law. The Norwegian dramatist, then already one of the great "literary powers" in Europe, was a very passionate man, always ready to defend his point of view with vigor, leaving no room for opposition. Understandably, Thoma did not find his attitude too appealing. A point of severe conflict between the two men was Björnson's view of the Germans as a nation of people infected with "corporal's mentality," as he called it. When Björnson discredited the German historian Theodor Mommsen and his *History of the Roman Empire*, Thoma reacted violently by calling the books of Björnson's favorite historian, the Italian professor Boni, "bullshit." However, Björnson forgave the "insolent German," and the two remained good friends.

The founder of the *Simplicissimus*, Albert Langen, was in the meantime living in exile in Switzerland. It must have been very difficult for the energetic man merely to watch the development of his own enterprise from the sidelines. But a return to Germany at that time would have meant certain imprisonment for him. Thoma defended Langen against accusations of cowardice, pointing out that the likely jail term would have entirely ruined the nervous little man's fragile health.[22] Reluctantly accepting the situation, Langen held periodic conferences with his staff in Constance or in Zürich while Thoma and Dr. Reinhold Geheeb carried the main load of administrative work in the editor's office in Munich. The work appealed to Thoma; and the relative freedom in scheduling his office hours meant a great deal to him. Another positive element was the congenial atmosphere among the staff members, who were all around thirty years old. During Langen's absence there was no real boss and matters were settled in mutual agreement. This was the type of job Thoma had desired for a long time, an occupation where duty was met by his inclinations, where work became play. The political events of the time, the main object of the *Simplicissimus's* satire, were by no means judged partially, since none of the contributors to the *Simplicissimus* was affiliated with a political party. Their common goal was to expose the weaknesses of political figures and of their supporters. Since the conservatives were in power and therefore played a decisive role in German politics, they and their head, Emperor Wilhelm II, became a natural target. As time went by, the *Simplicissimus's* criticism gradually took on the character of a crusade against the government and its "evil dealings." This development ultimately did more harm to the German state than the *Simplicissimus* people ever anticipated. During the last years of his life, Thoma questioned and even regretted the blind enthusiasm with which the *Simplicissimus* editors had dealt their heavy blows against the German establishment in these crucial years before World War I.[23] However, no one thought about a radicalization of politics, not to speak of the impending end of an epoch in history. Around the turn of the century it still seemed virtually impossible that the political constellation in Germany and in the world could ever change. Therefore, it seemed to be legitimate and healthy to attack a government which was archconservative and which acted stupidly on occasion. The writers of the *Simplicissimus* saw themselves as young, unprejudiced white knights out to fight the Philistines. They were in search of true freedom in a state where hypocrisy and suppression seemed to be the rule.

Retrospectively, it has to be said that the behavior of the German government toward the press was quite liberal, particularly during the last two decades of Wilhelm II's reign. But, after having experienced the trials surrounding the Palestine issue, the *Simplicissimus* people were of a different opinion. Although their articles appeared less belligerent during the weeks following Th. Th. Heine's sentencing, they soon began to show their teeth again. Their greatest satisfaction came not from the vocal applause of their friends all over Germany, but from the violent reactions of their foes. And the *Simplicissimus* acquired numerous enemies in a remarkably short time. Among them were the Catholic and the Protestant clergy, whose members made many attempts to bring about a general ban against the *Simplicissimus* to say nothing about the innumerable court injunctions which were served on motions by the churches. Cabinet ministers, attorneys, judges, police chiefs, and other high government officials were constantly on guard against the "destructive weekly." Even the law was stretched and bent, as in the Palestine issue, in order to curtail the activities of the *Simplicissimus's* editorial staff.[24]

A new target which presented itself to the sharp pencils of the *Simplicissimus's* satirists were the moral societies established to protect the German people against a supposedly galloping deterioration of morals. A puritanical wave began to sweep the country, vigorously encouraged by the clergy of both Christian denominations. At the occasion of a trial against a procurer in Berlin, the government proposed a bill for the protection of public morals, directed particularly against the freedom of the press. It was called *Lex Heinze*. As a reaction to the restrictions planned and partially executed by the government, the Goethe Society in Munich was founded by the writer Max Halbe and others. Writers like Georg Hirth and M. G. Conrad violently opposed the *Lex Heinze* in public. They finally saw the ominous bill killed in Parliament.

The death of this bill is another historic fact which can be seen as an example of the relative political tolerance in an era which has been widely interpreted as one of the dark periods, as far as human freedom and dignity are concerned.

Thoma had now established himself as a satirical writer and also as an efficient administrator. After some angry letters, Langen had agreed to publish his works. Thoma's books sold rather well on the German market, and within a few years he became a moderately wealthy man. Thanks to a vigorous sales campaign all over Germany, the *Simplicissimus* had also become a profitable enterprise. It had rapidly gained in popularity during the year 1900, when it attacked the British policy in South Africa which had led to the Boer War, a conflict which aroused violent protests all over Germany. As paradoxical as it seems, the *Simplicissimus* had become an "eye of the nation," despite its notorious criticism of the German government.

Very suddenly, in July 1901, Thoma decided to leave Munich and move to Berlin. In a letter to Langen, he explained the reasons for his abrupt departure.[25] A love affair had obviously become unbearable for the young writer; only an extended absence from Munich would provide a solution to the dilemma. After agreeing with Dr. Geheeb that he would manage the editorial office jointly with him *per distance*, he hastily left for the German capital. He had been in Berlin once before in spring of the same year, and the city had impressed him considerably. Now he enjoyed the legendary cultural life of the metropolis, and the theater performances in particular. He witnessed the unsuccessful premiere of Gerhart Hauptmann's *Der rote Hahn*, which ended in a full-fledged theater scandal. It did not take Thoma long to realize that no dramatist ruled Berlin at that time; the real potentates in the theater were the critics, who could make or break a writer at will. A notable exception in this conceited world of the Berlin theater was Otto Brahm, the director of the *Deutsches Theater*. He was known for his fairness vis-à-vis the dramatists whose plays he had accepted for performance, because he did not impose his will on them on every possible occasion during the rehearsals, as other directors were accustomed to doing. The quality of the performances given on his stage was known to be superb, mainly because he employed only excellent actors. Somewhat of a curiosity was the overwhelming success of an obscure play called *Alt Heidelberg*, a schmaltzy, operetta-style monstrosity set in an idealized student milieu, which no one in Berlin had dared to produce, afraid that the critics would tear it to pieces immediately. When it came out at the *Lessingtheater*, the public was in raptures about it. At first, the critics ignored the success of the romantic hodge-podge, but later generously agreed with the public. For once they had experienced the limits of their power.

In Hermann Sudermann, Thoma got to know a real poet. Although always a bit skeptical about famous men, he was immediately impressed by Sudermann's modest behavior and natural way of conducting a conversation.

The world of the stage was not all that interested Thoma during his stay in Berlin. He was also fascinated by the city itself, with its generous outlay, its clean streets, where beggars were never seen, its neat sidewalks, and its orderly traffic. He noted that at that time Berlin was many times larger than Munich, but incomparably better administered.

Also fascinating was the industry and economic success of the bourgeoisie in Berlin. But Thoma detected a peculiar kind of uneasiness and even reluctance to openly criticize the government and its institutions, even among people who stood close to the opposition. This special kind of subject loyalty he observed in action at the opening of an exhibition of the *Sezession*. Georg von Vollmar, a Munich artist, gave a speech after the dinner reception, in which he mildly attacked the staleness of the so-called "official art" which surrounded the Prussian court. There was friendly applause after the speech, but one could see silent embarrassment on many faces. Obviously, the guests' enthusiasm for modern art was not as serious as it had seemed, and Vollmar remarked to Thoma: "These people would like nothing better than to have the emperor present, who could say whatever he pleased about this 'gutter art,' and all of them would utterly enjoy it. . . ."[26] The accuracy of Vollmar's words was to be proven on the same day, since the Berlin press totally ignored his speech. In retrospect, Thoma assesses this as one of the symptoms of the unsound political climate in Germany around the turn of the century, in which even the liberal opposition kept silent in the face of incompetence and stupidity exhibited by officials of the government. Thoma puts the greatest share of the blame on the Social Democrats for overlooking this precarious state of affairs, which was soon to have a bearing even on German foreign policy by creating the image of the "ugly German" around the world. They managed to divert public attention from these vital issues by waging a massive campaign against the evils of capitalism, which manifested itself in spectacular polemics, capturing the people's eyes and ears.

In March 1902 Albert Langen, still not permitted to set foot on German soil, summoned his editors to a conference in Zürich, providing a welcome reason for Thoma to leave Berlin. The enthusiasm he had felt for the German capital only a year earlier had almost totally disappeared. And he was homesick for his beloved Bavaria and its mountains. After the Zürich conference, Langen invited Thoma to return with him to Paris, since there were some unresolved questions to discuss concerning the *Simplicissimus.* Thoma gladly accepted the invitation. He had wanted to see the city on the Seine for quite some time. Now, in Langen, who seemed to know just about everybody of importance in Paris, he had a most competent guide.

A visit to Rodin's atelier left a deep impression on Thoma. He was not only fascinated by the magnificent display of finished and unfinished masterworks, but even more by the outstanding personality of Rodin himself.

At one of Langen's dinner parties in Paris, Thoma met a former lieutenant colonel of the French army by the name of Picquart, who had become famous through his connection to the Dreyfus affair, a scandal which was still much talked about in public. A quiet man, Picquart was always one to listen to a conversation rather than to take part in it, even when he sat next to Paul Clémenceau, the brother of Georges Clémenceau. When Georges Clémenceau became prime minister in 1906, Picquart was appointed his minister of war. For the German army, Picquart had words of admiration because he had studied its organization.

In 1902, after Thoma had established himself as the leading

figure among the staff of the *Simplicissimus,* he rented the house of a Tegernsee farm family by the name of Six in Finsterwald for the summer. Viktor came along, of course, to enjoy the Upper Bavarian surroundings which she had missed for such a long time. Thoma's brother Peter, who had returned from Australia, and his sister Berta assisted in keeping the household. Thoma, the center of his "court" at Tegernsee, worked on a new stage play which he called *Lokalbahn* (Branch Line) and which was to become an overwhelming success. Frequently, friends and acquaintances interrupted the rural tranquillity of the farm. Living nearby was the well-known publisher Georg Hirth, the founder of *Jugend,* whom Thoma had admired since his Dachau days. Hirth and Thoma became close friends during these weeks in Finsterwald. A full-blooded journalist, Hirth had already made plans when he was twelve years old to establish a weekly paper. In 1858, he began to work for the *Westermanns Monatshefte,* probably the most famous cultural journal in the German-speaking countries. Having expressed his liberal views in numerous articles, he became a popular figure in Berlin's newspaper world. There he founded the *Annalen des Deutschen Reiches.* After later moving to Bavaria, he worked for the *Augsburger Allgemeine Zeitung* before taking over the publishing of the *Münchner Neueste Nachrichten.* He was among the founding members of the *Sezession,* an avant-garde society dedicated to new ideas and concepts in contemporary art. He must have been a physically attractive person. Thoma describes him as a man with an energetic-looking face, white hair, and expressive eyes.[27] In conversation, he immediately impressed his partners by the warmth he exuded and by the genuine kindness with which he spoke about people and things. At the same time, he had profound knowledge of the problems and conflicts of his times.

The summer over, Thoma returned to Munich, where his new comedy *Die Lokalbahn* had its premiere at the *Residenztheater.* "Old Viktor," who in the summer had attended the premiere of Thoma's first successful stage play, *Die Medaille,* was again among the audience. Dressed in her best for the festive occasion, she anxiously followed the performance up to the final, overwhelming applause. Naturally she took part in the "victory celebration" held afterwards at the restaurant Vier Jahreszeiten. In spite of a bad cold which she had caught this same evening, she traveled home to Allershausen on the next day. About a week later, having developed influenza, she died, after bidding a final farewell to "her Ludwig," who had rushed to her side. With the passing of "old Viktor," the last remaining link to Thoma's happy childhood in the Vorderriss was gone.

In January 1903 Thoma went to Vienna, where his *Lokalbahn* had been accepted for performance at the most famous of all German stages, the *Burgtheater*. He had truly come a long way to this evening of triumph. The premiere in Vienna had been preceded by a very successful one at the theater in Stuttgart. But, as Thoma stood alone behind a column of the opulent *Burgtheater* watching the equipages arrive, a strange feeling of indifference, amidst the evening's glamor, overcame him. All of the people who had meant most to him were dead. Nobody around him really cared about the success or failure of his play. With deep sadness he imagined his mother seeing him as the celebrated author of a play about to be performed at the famous imperial stage, something which certainly would have meant the realization of many of her dreams.

Following the premiere, Thoma celebrated the successful performance over a glass of Pilsner beer with Paul Schlenther, the director of the *Burgtheater*. Schlenther was amazed by the extreme calm with which he had seen Thoma follow the performance. But the real reasons for his seeming lack of concern remained known only to Thoma.

During his stay in Vienna, Thoma was introduced to several men who at that time played important roles in Vienna's public life. He got to know Karl Schönherr as a quiet North Tyrolian who talked as little as men from the Tyrolian Inn Valley normally do. Another peculiar individual, a species of which Vienna seems to have produced a stately number, was Engelbert Pernerstorfer, a well-known Socialist politician. When he guided Thoma through the halls of the Parliament, being followed by threatening looks from the conservative and German national deputies, he reminded Thoma with great vigor that the Austrians in Upper and Lower Austria, as well as in Styria and Carinthia, were genuine Bavarians, just like the ones in "Old Bavaria." Although this was unmistakably true, it sounded strange to Thoma, coming from a well-known Socialist. In a little essay which he devoted to Pernerstorfer, Thoma calls him "a social democratic leader, but not a Social Democrat, neither in his character, nor in his inclinations, nor in his appearance."[28]

Among the other Viennese celebrities whom Thoma met were Karl Kraus, the satirist and dedicated pacifist; Peter Altenberg; Paul

Busson; and the poet F. David, who on being introduced recited several of Thoma's satirical poems from memory to show the author how popular he was in Vienna.

Slowly the melancholy which had overcome Thoma at the occasion of the *Burgtheater* premiere disappeared in the carefree *Gemütlichkeit* of old Vienna, the imperial city he had admired since his childhood days from pictures he had seen in *Über Land und Meer*. Even during his Traunstein days, he had envied the travelers he saw passing by on the express train to Vienna while he stood on the railway platform. Now he was walking the venerable streets in the heart of the city and could say to himself that life had given him more than it had promised. On this conciliatory note, he left Vienna.

Returning to Munich, Thoma found a lot of work waiting in the editor's office, since Langen was still absent. Thoma also had to keep up his reputation as an established writer. He did so splendidly by producing the *Lausbubengeschichten* and the short story "Der heilige Hies" during the year 1903.

After "old Viktor" died, Thoma began to feel very lonely, having lost the last person reminding him of "home." The months following her death saw the beginning of his friendship with Ludwig Ganghofer, one of the most celebrated novelists in Germany. The two men had many things in common. Both were of "old-Bavarian" background—their grandfathers had even been friends—and they shared a great passion for hunting. Thoma wonders in his memoirs why the two had not become friends earlier. His own explanation is that in Munich, unlike in Berlin or in Vienna, everybody lived like an island unto himself.[29] Now that the ice was finally broken, the two spent a few weeks together at the hunting lodge Hubertus, situated in a picturesque North Tyrolian valley, not far from the Vorderriss. Many things there reminded Thoma of his childhood. Every day the two men went hunting in the surrounding valleys and mountain forests, usually from early morning until nightfall. Sometimes when the weather was so bad that they could not find their way back to the lodge, they stayed in a primitive shelter high up in the mountains. It was the kind of life Thoma needed in order to regain his vigor. Even later, after he was married and conflicts began within the marriage, he came to Hubertus when he needed to get away from the quarrels.

In 1903, Thoma met Ignatius Taschner, a sculptor who became his best friend. Taschner was a gifted, ingenious little fellow from

Lohr on the Main River, where his father had been a stonemason. As a boy in his father's shop, he had learned to see a piece of art as one unit, just as the great masters of the Middle Ages had, while at the same time he had learned to plan a work to the smallest detail, as a craftsman must. He began as an apprentice in a painting shop in Schweinfurt, then studied at the Academy of Arts in Munich, where his talent startled his teachers; and after completing several major commissions in Bavaria, he was offered a professorship at Breslau. There he stayed until 1905, when he moved to Berlin, where he produced most of his well-known works. In Mitterndorf near Dachau he built his home, where he spent as much time as his profession would allow. After a life of fulfilling work, he died in 1913, only forty-two years old. Taschner's death mask hangs over the desk in the study at the "Tuften," Thoma's estate at Tegernsee, where he lived after 1908. The bronze crucifix at Thoma's grave in the churchyard of Rottach-Egern is a work of Ignatius Taschner, and so are the blueprints of Thoma's house at the "Tuften," as well as the illustrations to "Der heilige Hies." Among Taschner's numerous creations are a memorial statue of Friedrich Schiller in the city of Saint Paul, Minnesota; the table silver for the Prussian crown prince; and the fairy-tale fountain in Berlin. He was an artist of extraordinary imagination, both in his universality and in his skills, reminiscent of the medieval masters.

The spring of 1903 brought a welcome change of scenery. Together with Wilke, Heine, and Thöny, Thoma embarked on a bicycle tour of Italy, visiting Milan and Genoa first, and then traveling along the Riviera. On the way back, the group spent about six weeks in Pisa and Florence. Thoma took such a liking to the Mediterranean landscape and its convivial, simple people that he visited Italy each spring until the beginning of World War I. But never again did Italy give him so much pleasure as during this first visit of 1903. As impressed as he was by the rocky coastline of the Riviera with its picturesque fishing villages, he found the "vanity fair" of Monaco and its casinos disappointing.[30]

Thoma was enchanted by the untouched beauty of the Appenine valleys and by the friendly people of the region who were curious to hear from the visitors about the strange, cold country in the North. After their arrival in Florence, Thoma and his friends quickly learned how to spend their days in *dolce far niente*. They visited museums, ate rich Italian dinners, smoked black Toscana cigars, and drank delicious red country wine. It was a special entertain-

ment for the foursome to watch the typical German tourists, obliged
to spend their time looking at art objects. In Thoma's "Familie in
Italien," one can find a biting caricature of the German tourists in
southern Europe.[31] He found the traveling habits of the British and
American tourists even worse than those of the Germans. They were
like slaves to their hotel dinner schedules and were more interested
in jam for their muffins than Italy's art. Thoma himself never found
it necessary to follow Baedeker's instructions for tourists when he
visited the museums because he had the most competent Cicerones
with him, namely Heine and Wilke. As was to be expected, Thoma
and his friends got used to the slow pace of life in the South, and
they prepared their contributions for the *Simplicissimus* only reluctantly. The laziest of all was Wilke, who started work on a new cartoon only after repeated threats of curtailment of money, food, and
chianti. Before their departure from Italy, a banquet was given for
the *Simplicissimus* artists by the son of Arnold Böcklin.

While still in Florence, news had reached the travelers that
Langen had returned to Germany. Upon their return to Munich,
they found him full of plans and as lively and energetic as ever. He
had hired a new artist for the *Simplicissimus*, the Norwegian
draftsman Olaf Gulbransson. According to Langen's plans,
Gulbransson would begin by undertaking intensive studies of the
German milieu in Berlin. Gulbransson disliked the city so
thoroughly that Langen had to bring him back to Munich. He arrived there in January 1903, just as the "carnival" was getting under
way. The Norwegian immediately involved himself with great
enthusiasm in planning and executing the festivities, still not able to
speak German at all. He got so attached to Munich that he decided
to stay in the Bavarian capital. He later became a real Bavarian in
dialect and habits. Gulbransson's famous caricature portraying
Thoma with a few rough lines, holding a big peasant's pipe, became
the best-known picture of Ludwig Thoma.

The winters of 1902 and 1903 were jovial times for the artists of
the *Simplicissimus*. One masked ball followed another, and
evenings were filled with jokes, fun, and drinking. In one
photograph taken at the veterans' ball in the Arzberger Keller in
Munich, Thoma may be seen posing as Prince Bismarck, his friends
at his side dressed as Prussian soldiers, as if to celebrate the victory
of 1870.

During the winter of 1904, Thoma visited "Ignaz" Taschner in
Nuremberg, where the artist happened to be taking care of business

matters. On the occasion of a visit to the House of Faber, Thoma made the acquaintance of a charming young lady who immediately captured his attention. She was Maidi Feist-Belmont, the daughter of a wealthy champagne manufacturer in Frankfurt am Main. The pretty young girl also took a liking to the robust-looking Bavarian who wrote stage plays and satirical poems. In the summer of 1905, Maidi and her mother visited Thoma in his hideout in Finsterwald. Thoma never found the courage to propose marriage to Maidi that summer, and the two did not meet again until almost fourteen years later. In countless letters to Maidi, which followed the renewal of their friendship, Thoma expressed regret about his earlier hesitation. The young lawyer and writer had never been a ladies' man, and in the company of Maidi, who was quite some years younger but whom he admired sincerely from the first moment, he must have been exceptionally bashful. In a letter written to Maidi in 1918, he revealed the impression she had made on him at their first meeting: it was as if "[my dead] mother was standing beside me, and it seemed to me that she was saying, 'This one you must marry.' "[32] In 1906, the Feist-Belmonts again spent the summer at Tegernsee. But by then Thoma was in Berlin, and already married to someone else.

After returning from a second extensive bicycle tour, taken in the spring of 1904 with Thöny and Wilke through southern Europe and North Africa, Thoma began working on his first long narrative, *Andreas Vöst*, a tragic novel set in the Bavarian peasant milieu, which stirred up considerable political dust when it appeared in 1905. The conservatives saw a deliberate attack against them in the way Thoma presented one of the main figures of the book, the clergyman who manages to ruin the life of a farmer who had refused to obey his orders. But Thoma's reputation as a writer was already undisputed. When the *Münchner Neueste Nachrichten* bought the rights to print his novel in daily installments, Thoma could command a salary of twelve thousand marks.

To celebrate the novel's overwhelming success, Thoma gave a dinner party in his Munich apartment. Among the guests were Langen, Hirth, Geheeb, Holm, Wilke, and a very pretty young woman—one might even say an exotic beauty—by the name of Marietta di Rigardo. Langen and his friends had brought her along as a conversation partner for their host, who up to then had appeared more interested in hunting and in his books than in female company. Since he was about to become financially independent, there was growing fear among his friends on the *Simplicissimus* that he might move away from Munich and into a remote Alpine valley. They certainly could not afford to lose their most effective contributor, and so one can easily understand their attempt to interest him in this beautiful creature, who, it was hoped, would keep him in Munich.

It would be hard to imagine two more different individuals in appearance and in background than Thoma and Marietta, or Marion, as he was later used to calling her. Marion was a tiny, fragile person with a dark complexion, black hair, and very dark eyes. When she appeared in public, she immediately attracted everyone's attention because of her exotic looks. And she indeed was of exotic origin. Her father was a Swiss-born hotel receptionist in the Philippines, her mother was from India. Marion was born in Manila, but educated in Switzerland, and, after finishing school she became a dancer. When Thoma met her, she was married to a man who was suffering from a lung ailment, and from whom she was contemplating a divorce. Her overwhelming charm and beauty, and her open defiance of all convention and tradition fascinated Thoma. Almost immediately he began to see in her the woman of his life. He thought of her as a child of nature who could understand him and make him happy, better than a daughter from a "good family" might ever have been able to.

During the summer of 1905, Thoma and Marion spent many days together playing tennis, hiking, or swimming. For the first time in his life, Thoma was completely happy in the company of a woman. The formalities of Marion's divorce seemed to take endless time. But at the beginning of September, Marion was free, and the two were able to marry. Berlin and Vienna were the stops on the honeymoon. In Vienna, Karl Kraus, whom Thoma had met at the premiere of his *Lokalbahn*, played host to the newlyweds, who were rushed from one reception and gala dinner in their honor to another. A stay at the nearby Semmering Mountain resort ended these exhilarating but turbulent weeks. Thoma felt as if he had conquered the world.

In Munich, the Thomas moved into an elegant apartment on the Leopoldstrasse, which they cozily furnished with antique furniture and objects of folk art. But the city was not able to hold Thoma for very long. He was soon to be found hunting in the mountains around the Tegernsee, or in the Dachau district where he shared hunting rights with Langen.

The year 1906 brought important changes in Thoma's professional life. First, although more by force than by persuasion, the artists of the *Simplicissimus* finally convinced Langen that the *Simplicissimus* should be run as a corporation. They saw profits on the rise and did not want to remain slaves at the mercy of an "almighty" publisher. After all, they were the ones who were largely responsible for the success of the *Simplicissimus*. Thoma was in agreement with the demands of the other major contributors, but he did not condone the rather tactless manner in which they presented their ultimatum to the startled Langen. The second development was the creation of an entirely new periodical, completely independent of the *Simplicissimus*, but also published by Albert Langen. Thoma and Hermann Hesse were the editors of the new publication, which they called *März*, although the original plan was to name it *Süddeutschland*. *März* focused on issues dealing with cultural life in the South of Germany. Thoma had been the first to point out that a regional cultural periodical was needed since the *Simplicissimus* had shown how difficult it was to please Berlin, Leipzig, Cologne, Stuttgart, and Munich at the same time. Among Thoma's contributions to *März* one finds mainly essays of a political nature, very serious in tone, unlike his articles and poems in the *Simplicissimus*. A few years later, Theodor Heuss, who became West Germany's first Federal president after World War II, took over the editorship of the biweekly.

The year 1906 had more in store for Ludwig Thoma than mere changes in his professional life. Enraged by the hypocrisy of the German moral societies, and of some Protestant clergymen, he wrote an extremely satirical poem for the *Simplicissimus* entitled "An die Moralprediger zu Köln am Rheine" (To the Moral Preachers in Cologne on the Rhine), in which he most eloquently attacks the Protestant ministers who condemn the "evils of sex" from the pulpit, but who indulge in the same "evils" behind the closed doors of their homes. Vicious outcries denouncing "Peter Schlemihl" as a sacrilegist went through the conservative press of the North. A lawsuit was filed against Thoma, since by then everyone knew that he was "Peter Schlemihl," and he had to appear before a court in Stuttgart. The trial received massive publicity, since such well-known public figures as Ludwig Ganghofer vigorously intervened (he once pounded his fist on the judge's table during the trial). The judges, somewhat startled by all the vocal opposition, reacted by sentencing Thoma to six weeks in jail. A wave of jubilant cries went out through parts of the German press: "Peter Schlemihl" had finally met justice. During a convention dealing with public morals, which took place in Magdeburg, a royal court preacher from Berlin thanked Fate for punishing this most "destructive" journalist. In October, after the hunting season was over, Thoma delivered himself to the state prison in Munich / Stadelheim to serve his sentence. He had turned down an offer made by the authorities, who had raised the possibility of amnesty had he been willing to submit an appeal for mercy. But for Thoma an acceptance of the offer would have equaled an admission of guilt, and, at the same time, would not have permitted him to write further attacks. He preferred to go to jail rather than to promise to become an "obedient subject."

The loneliness of prison presented the worst torture for Thoma. He tried to ease his restlessness through extensive reading of Raabe, Scribe, Plato, and historical literature, and he read with greatest pleasure about the coup of a jobless shoemaker in Berlin who had posed as an army officer, thus triggering the famous "Captain of Köpenick" affair. More and more enraged at the sanctimonious behavior of the "apostles of morality," Thoma began to formulate plans for a new comedy which was to administer a more massive blow to the double standards of their strange ethics. It appeared two years later, in 1908, under the title *Moral*. After a few weeks of confinement, Thoma began to feel his energies dwindling. The prison atmosphere had begun to undermine his spirit, and a certain lethargy overcame him. Visitors like Langen and Kurt Aram, one of Thoma's new colleagues in the editorial office of *März*, noticed signs of depression in Thoma's face, which had begun to take on a gray pallor. They smuggled in a little paperback, taken apart to prevent discovery, containing the speeches of Emperor Wilhelm II, which had just been published by Reclam in Leipzig. It was the right medicine for the unhappy man. The emperor's speeches, full of trite phrases and commonplaces, started Thoma's adrenalin flowing and, in a serious article published later in *März*, he berated the shallowness of Wilhelm's public statements, which he described as mere "noise"; and deplored the foolishness of the publishers who had printed them.

During the last two weeks of his stay in Stadelheim prison, something much closer to his heart occupied Thoma: the plans for a house of his own, to be built after plans drafted by his friend Taschner. During the previous summer, Thoma had already selected and acquired a beautiful piece of land, which he called "Tuften," located above Rottach at the southeast corner of the Tegernsee. The parcel was large enough to support the operation of a small dairy farm, which was to be run by a caretaker who would live in a small outbuilding. Thoma happily considered Taschner's careful studies of sun, wind, and weather conditions in the little valley, but thoughts about the house and farm only helped to make him more restless behind the prison walls.

On November 27, 1906, Thoma was finally released from Stadelheim and was met outside by a small group of friends. He and Marion celebrated his freedom with a lavish dinner. Before long, Thoma was again in the mountains, hunting and skiing, enjoying the outdoors as never before in his life. He had learned what it meant to be confined behind walls.

The next year, 1907, was, in Thoma's own words, a "lazy year."[33] Aside from caring for the development of *März*, his main concern was building the house on the "Tuften" in Rottach. During construction, it became apparent that the execution of Taschner's design would be quite expensive. Although he drew a nice monthly income, Thoma's finances began to be strained. But Langen, his boss, showed true generosity by advancing Thoma eight thousand marks toward the completion of the building. He knew he would not be disappointed in Thoma. And, indeed, Thoma's new comedy, *Moral*, turned out the following year, became a best-seller, bringing in more than a million marks in royalties within a very short time.

In May 1908 Thoma moved into his new house, which was to become the center of his life, the point on the globe to which he could always return. And how similar the house on the "Tuften" was to the one in the Vorderriss! It was situated at the entrance of a lovely valley, and mountain ranges with dark spruce forests on their slopes looked down on it from all sides. Looking out from its windows one still sees today green meadows dotted with bright and colorful Alpine flowers. Inside the house one finds the same spaciousness there had been in the forester's house. There is a broad hall on both the first and second floors, and the large living room is furnished as a so-called *Bauernstube*, in the typical peasant style with rugged furniture and a carved wooden crucifix mounted on the wall in the corner above the table. Thoma called it his "*Häusl*" (little house), but it is really a very stately mansion.

On the third floor, Thoma set up his study, a large, Spartan-looking room with a rather low ceiling. A relatively small desk, built

in the Biedermeier style, stands in the center. Facing the desk
stands a bookcase, with glass doors, containing all the volumes of
März, bound in leather. The opposite wall contains Thoma's private
library, consisting mainly of German classical literature including
the works of Lessing, Goethe, Keller, and Stifter. There are also
works on economics and some law books. From the northeast side of
the room, one can step out onto a wooden balcony, where Thoma
usually relaxed after he had finished his daily *pensum* of writing. It
is in this room, on the wall near the window, that the death mask of
Ignatius Taschner hangs.

Thoma saw deep meaning in the ownership of a home and of
land which could be useful in producing food. In a letter to Conrad
Haussmann, he expressed this concept in a unique way.[34] Farming
on his own land showed him the relative value of things, and
sometimes he came to the conclusion that a few pounds of cow
manure used as fertilizer for a small area of soil achieved a lot more
than he, the essayist, did with some of his articles which were pack-
ed with "wisdom." This comparison, rustic as it may sound, shows
through Thoma's ability to make fun of his own work, how truly
modest this man was. Thoma deeply respected and understood the
mentality of the farmer who is able to distinguish the real priorities.
Mind and body must be kept in balance, and, for Thoma, this was
best achieved through life in the country.

Once settled in his new house, Thoma found no difficulty starting
to write again after the "lazy" year which preceded the move. In
1908 he completed two major works in rapid succession: the comedy, *Moral*; and the satire in prose, *Briefwechsel eines bayerischen
Landtagsabgeordneten* (Correspondence of a Bavarian Deputy), the
so-called *Filserbriefe* (Filser Letters).

The plans for *Moral* had already had been worked out while
Thoma was in Stadelheim prison. The comedy turned out to be a
demolishing broadside against the hypocrites in the moral societies
who had been instrumental in putting Thoma behind bars. Two
premieres initiated the triumphant stage career of *Moral*. One took
place in Berlin on November 20, 1908, and the other in Munich one
day later. After each of these performances, the audiences showered
the author with applause. Performances on all of the major stages in
Germany followed, the most spectacular one in Stuttgart, where the
public had always been friendly to Thoma. Literally overnight,
Thoma had become a dramatist of the first order.

Moral made Thoma a wealthy man within a remarkably short

time. He never again had financial worries and was able to pay off the mortgages and advances on the house in Rottach and thereafter afford to live a life of leisure. Since Thoma could now spend more time at home on the Tegernsee, most of the burden of the *Simplicissimus's* editorial work had to be shared by Korfiz Holm and Dr. Geheeb. But Thoma by no means became a hermit. Every year, before the outbreak of World War I, he spent several weeks in Italy and France. There was never any thought of leaning back in triumph, or of enjoying idleness. Nor did he intend to dig in and become a farmer, although the caricatures of him drawn by his friend Gulbransson made him look like one. He remained the alert and sensitive guardian of the moral and political consciousness of his country and of his time until the end of his life. Success could not corrupt his strong character.

The *Briefwechsel eines bayerischen Landtagsabgeordneten* became another big success for Thoma. These highly satirical fictional letters of a deputy in the Bavarian parliament were aimed at the conservative Bavarian Center party which, guided by members of the clergy, dominated the Bavarian political scene in the first decade of our century. Even today, although the issues which were the subject of the letters have long been obsolete, one cannot refrain from laughing when reading the *Filserbriefe*, if for no other reason than because of the incredibly faulty spelling Thoma contrived for them. When published in 1908, the irresistible humor in these letters had an explosive effect.

Thoma was very happy in his new home at the "Tuften." But Marion Thoma did not share these feelings. She had wept on the day before they moved into the new house, fearing that she would live a life of solitude and isolation in the new environment. Her habitat had always been the world of the stage, of ballrooms and cocktail parties. She needed people around her to admire her and to provide constant excitement. Naturally, her gregariousness led to a conflict with Thoma, who sought the peace and tranquillity of the mountains. At the beginning, he overlooked Marion's flighty bearing and labeled it childish. But soon her restless nature became unbearable for him. He had wanted a stable comrade, a wife with whom he could share his interests and hobbies. Her absences from the "Tuften" became increasingly longer, and occasionally Thoma heard from friends that Marion had been seen in the company of other men. This hurt Thoma deeply, but he did not show his grief to her when she returned. He more and more adapted himself to the role of a father and protector rather than a husband. Already in 1908, he must have resigned himself to this new reality. Then, in 1910, he openly told Marion that he would be merely her friend from then on, if she wanted that. When she did not return to the Tegernsee after this serious appeal, Thoma submitted the divorce papers. The divorce was granted in the spring of 1911. Thoma was again free, but his correspondence with Marion did not immediately cease. For years he tried to be a consulting friend. Then, in 1918, he stopped further communication with her after he had heard worse things about her than ever before. He no longer wanted her to be mentioned in association with him.

The year 1909 was a very sad one for Thoma. Besides the increasing differences with his wife, he had to bear several losses that were even more painful for him than the breakup of his marriage. In April, Albert Langen suddenly died. A passionate motorist, the little man had caught an infection of the inner ear while riding in his open automobile. He had neglected the symptoms of the ailment at first, and when the pain became unbearable, it was already too late for an operation. Quietly, he settled his estate and died, only thirty-nine years old. Thoma's relations with Langen had not always been free of tensions or even quarrels, but he had come to know the nervous but always optimistic man as a true friend, who had been the personification of tolerance and of progress during all the years Thoma had known him, since 1897. In *Leute, die ich kannte*, Thoma warmly remembers Langen, his friend and mentor, in an essay dedicated to him.[35]

Only one month later, Ferdinand von Reznicek, the ingenious artist from Austria, also died suddenly. Shortly afterwards, Rudolf Wilke succumbed as well. It was difficult for Thoma to believe that within a very short period of time he had lost people whom he had counted among his very best friends. He felt that part of his own life had vanished with them. The old enthusiasm and conviviality which had always dominated the atmosphere at the *Simplicissimus* in Munich were now gone. Everything was more serious and less inspiring. In a letter to Ganghofer, Thoma mourned the death of his friends and looked back on the decade which had just passed. It had certainly been the most eventful time in his life.[36]

After 1909, Thoma began to be an increasingly lonely man, spending most of his time at the "Tuften." He was in communication with only a few, selected men, like Ganghofer and Conrad

Haussmann. He had reached the climax of his life. The turbulent times were over, and it was his intention to bring in the harvest in his remaining years. He would only have a little more than ten years to accomplish this task.

IV *Harvest*

The year 1910 marked a new beginning in several ways. First of all, Thoma finally realized that his marriage to Marion was on a hopeless course, and that it was time to cut ties with her. Although frequently plagued with feelings of loneliness, he preferred the life of a bachelor to following his wife from party to party. After this difficult situation had been resolved, he was able to return to work.

Thoma's eagerness to finish a new comedy bore fruit within the same year: *Erster Klasse* is, without any doubt, his finest play. It probably also holds the record of performances among his dramas. It represents an episode out of Joseph Filser's journey to Munich, where the legislative period of the Diet was about to begin. Filser, whom nobody suspects of being a deputy of the Parliament, sparks off an argument with some of the other passengers. The play was an overwhelming success when it appeared, and it remains highly popular in our day as well.

During 1910, Thoma's friendship with Ludwig Ganghofer intensified. Thoma had come to realize that this man was the only friend besides Ignatius Taschner with whom a deep understanding was possible. In a letter written November 16, 1910, he revealed his feelings to Ganghofer.[37] He also let his friend know that he was entangled in a new literary project, which was to result in one of his most expressive works. The story had to do with the fate of a Bavarian peasant farmer whose wife suddenly dies, leaving him alone to operate the farm; and a son, who is jealous of the household's female servant, who has designs on the father. Thoma called the novel *Der Wittiber* (Widower). Its great success is mainly founded in its precise language and in the striking realism with which the author describes the peasant milieu.

In April 1911 Thoma traveled to France. He stayed in Paris for a few weeks, where he had plenty of opportunities to revive old acquaintances and memories. Spring in Paris had always meant something special to him since the days of his first stay in the metropolis on the Seine more than ten years earlier.

Since 1908 Thoma had been familiarizing himself with the works
of the Austrian writer Ludwig Anzengruber, one of the most
successful dramatists during the years before World War I. Several
of his plays are designated *Volksstücke* (popular plays). These are
dramas in which dialect is used extensively. Their plot is set in a
popular milieu, and they usually end in tragedy. Highly effective on
the stage, this kind of play enjoyed great popularity with the public
for a long period of time. When Thoma began reading
Anzengruber's plays, which had been written in the seventies and
which had become such great successes, they were more than a
quarter-century old. He became increasingly certain that a new
Volksstück was needed on the German stage. In the fall of 1911, he
began to work on *Magdalena*, a peasant tragedy which he finished
during spring of the following year. In October 1912 the premiere
took place in Berlin. Thoma attended in the company of a number
of friends, including Michel Dengg, an actor who contributed
significantly to the success of Thoma's plays on stage. Before the
evening of the premiere, Thoma once again fell into a spell of
melancholy, very similar to the one he had experienced in Vienna
before the performance of *Lokalbahn* at the *Burgtheater*. His spirits
were only momentarily brightened when he passed by the fairy-tale
fountain of Ignatius Taschner, in front of the city hall in
Friedrichshain. During the performance, Marion sat beside the
author, attending the premiere in spite of their recent separation.
The performance of *Magdalena* must have been brilliant, and the
applause most generous. Even the "almighty" critic Alfred Kerr
praised *Magdalena* in his column, commending the author for having created a drama which had clearly broken the boundaries of the
Volksstück, and which had reached into the sphere of genuine
tragedy.

The greatest triumph came a week later when *Magdalena* was
performed at the *Residenztheater* in Munich. After the premiere,
the audience gave Thoma a long ovation. As much as the Berlin
public had been moved by the tragedy, the Bavarian dialect had
certainly been an obstacle to their ability to identify with the figures
of the play to the utmost extent. In Munich, however, the dialect
acted as a ferment which heightened the dramatic tension and
magnified the effect of the catastrophe on the spectator. *Magdalena*
was a redounding success.

The second half of the *Filserbriefe* appeared during 1912. They
represent a continuation of Filser's reports about the new legislative

session. During the same year, Thoma wrote several little stories, all of which appeared in 1913, depicting everyday Bavarian life, e.g., "Unser guater, alter Herzog Karl" (Our Good Old Duke Karl), "Auf der Elektrischen" (On the Streetcar), "Auf dem Bahnsteig" (At the Station Platform), and others. In the same year, he published a small volume entitled *Münchner Karneval* (Munich Carnival), containing poems he had written for the *Simplicissimus*, and which were illustrated by his friend Reznicek. There was also a new play dealing with social prejudices, feminine equality, and several other issues of the day, which Thoma called *Die Sippe* (The Clan). The play was not as great a success on stage as was his next comedy, *Das Säuglingsheim* (Infants' Asylum), which attacks religious prejudices and bureaucratic clumsiness.

In November 1913 Thoma suffered another great loss. His best friend, Ignatius Taschner, suddenly died, not yet forty-three years old. Thoma missed Taschner more than anyone he had ever known, except his parents. Between the two men there had prevailed not only a deep mutual admiration of their art, but also a profound understanding of minds. Thoma would never know anyone who was able to match Taschner's solidity and character again. In a letter to Karl Rothmaier, Thoma expressed his regard for his dead friend as an artist and as a human being:

For me, the Franconian *Altmeister* ["old master"] Taschner, who was an Old Bavarian of the best breed, stands alongside of the truly great Gothic masters, and it is of great value to me that I learned to understand his art, which embraced great and small things equally. One hour with [Taschner], who was gifted with the most infallible judgment, was more valuable than the reading of whole volumes. . . . How he, as a cordial man and as a universal artist, still remained a child, how his personality was the most charming, how his blend of deep seriousness and dear roguishness captured me again and again, that I will one day tell you.[38]

V   *War*

On June 28, 1914, Archduke Franz Ferdinand of Austria was assassinated in Sarajevo. Exactly one month later, Austria declared war on Serbia. On August 1, 1914, Germany entered the war. One day earlier, Thoma had taken part in a meeting at the *Simplicissimus* and had gone hunting to Weikersfelden, near Dachau. He was on his way back to the Tegernsee when he heard about the general mobilization at the train station in Munich. Riding home on

the train, he looked out of the window and saw the peaceful
Bavarian landscape and industrious farmers just finishing a long
summer day's work. The thought that war was now a fact,
something he had feared for years, seemed inconceivable to him.
But the thought officially became reality on the same day, at 7:00
P.M., when Germany declared war on Russia.

Much has been said about Thoma's sudden change in political
conviction, which now followed. Many who had read his grim
satires against the emperor and the establishment in general
thought that Thoma had betrayed himself. Nothing was further
from the truth.

Thoma was an honest man all of his life, and he lived like one,
too. When he saw the peaceful lives of all the small farmers around
him threatened by foreign powers, the choice was very clear for
him. After all, he had never fought against the people in his articles,
but had only opposed their government, with its pompous gestures
and its shallow phrases. Now, since the war had started, all opposition had to stop. Germany, this wonderful country full of industrious and ingenious people, was in danger of falling victim to
the greed of evil powers who had always been jealous of its growth
and success. For Thoma there were no longer any enemies among
the Germans; the enemies were abroad. Everything humanly possible had to be done to prevent Germany from losing the war.

A few days after the outbreak of the war, Thoma told the other
members of the *Simplicissimus's* editorial staff that the time of the
Simplicissimus was over, that the magazine should be abolished. In
wartime, there could be no place for criticism of one's country.
However, Th. Th. Heine was able to change Thoma's mind by
arguing that instead of closing shop, the *Simplicissimus* should
vigorously represent the side of the German government. It was indeed vital that a publication of the international reputation that the
Simplicissimus had enjoyed should explain the German point of
view.

Thoma was determined to serve his embattled fatherland. A
satirical article which he had written for *März*, dealing with the
time before and after 1848, was immediately withdrawn.[39] To
Conrad Haussmann he expressed admiration for the young recruits
who were leaving their farms to fight for Germany.[40] Thoma himself had volunteered twice, on July 31 and on August 2, 1914, for
service in the Bavarian medical corps, since he was too old for com-
bat duty. But it took the bureaucrats in Munich a long time even to

consider his request. Finally, in the fall of 1914, he was granted permission to distribute gift parcels containing mainly tobacco and snuff to the troops in the Vosges Mountains. In the spring of 1915, he was detached to a truck convoy at the Western Front as a medic. Himself always in good spirits, Thoma had conquered the hearts of the whole company within a few days. On April 24, 1915, the convoy was ordered to the Russian Front, where an offensive was being mounted which later led to the breakthrough at Gorlice in Galicia. Days and nights filled with the sounds of battle and the cries of the wounded followed. On June 6, 1915, Thoma received the Iron Cross for his services in the field. Soon after that, he felt increasing pains in the digestive tract, which turned out to be dysentery. On June 16, 1915, he left the Eastern Front on home leave, hoping to be back after ten days. At the beginning of August, he served near Brest Litovsk, but he had to return home soon because of a new attack of dysentery. In spite of severe pain and a constant feeling of nausea, Thoma did not want to give up his own effort to help in the war. In November 1917 he undertook a trip to the Italian Front, still wearing the uniform of an army medic.

Ludwig Ganghofer also endorsed the German war effort with great enthusiasm. He traveled as a war correspondent, cheering up the troops wherever he appeared. But Ganghofer's tours of the fronts were criticized and even ridiculed by the press at home in cartoons, mainly because Ganghofer was one of the emperor's favorite writers. Karl Kraus has Ganghofer appear in a humorous scene of his drama *Die letzten Tage der Menschheit* (The Last Days of Mankind).

Thoma saw no justification for jokes which downgraded Germany and its patriots. When he talked about his fatherland, his voice took on a sharp tone. In a public appeal to buy war bonds, made in 1917, he warned the people that they would have to make financial sacrifices in order to save Germany and to secure the future of their children. Before he published his appeal, he himself bought war bonds in the amount of fifty thousand marks, a sum which represented his entire cash savings.

The war occupied Thoma's mind almost entirely, and his literary output was small. Before he went to the front in 1915, he had finished a one-act comedy entitled *Der alte Feinschmecker* (The Old Connoisseur). This was followed by *Die kleinen Verwandten* (The Small Inlaws), *Dichters Ehrentag* (Writer's Day of Honor), and others. During the long months of convalescence from dysentery in

1916, he finished *Onkel Peppi* (Uncle Peppi), a masterful little piece of prose, using social differences as the source of various humorous events. Thoma also started *Heilige Nacht* (Holy Night), an epic poem, in which he tells the story of Christ's birth, using the regional dialect spoken in and around Lenggries. Weakened by the long ailment, Thoma began to see an increasingly dark future ahead. Prevented from contributing to a German victory at the front, he began to lament his country's fate. The Bavarian essayist Josef Hofmiller became a frequent partner in Thoma's dialogues on German history which were carried on in the house at the "Tuften." Hofmiller's attempts to take Thoma's mind off the sad events of the present failed essentially. At the end of these long afternoons which the two spent in discussion, Thoma would always return to the one historical event which for him had marked the beginning of the end for Germany: Bismarck's forced retirement.

During the year 1917, when people began to realize that Germany would lose the war, Thoma started writing his memoirs, *Erinnerungen* (Recollections), which were published after his death, as was his *Stadelheimer Tagebuch* (Stadelheim Diary). In the last pages of this long essay, one experiences the repentance Thoma felt in remembering the vicious attacks he had launched against the state and its representatives ten years earlier. He felt guilty because he believed he had indirectly contributed to Germany's dilemma.

Conrad Haussmann was one of the partners in Thoma's political and historical discussions, which were carried out in letters. Thoma no longer agreed with Haussmann's democratic convictions, but he still honored him as a wise politician and as a friend. Haussmann had recommended Theodor Heuss as the editor of *März* to follow Thoma and Hesse, for which Thoma was very grateful, and he had also represented Thoma in several court cases connected with *Simplicissimus* articles.

During 1917, Thoma began working in *Altaich*, a broad and slow-moving story about a small Bavarian town which discovers tourism, enthusiastically indulges in it, and then returns to its old ways after the townspeople have experienced its dubious blessings. *Altaich* seems to be a little portrait of Traunstein as Thoma saw it in his younger days.

After the German Empire finally began to show the signs of defeat in the summer of 1918, Thoma met Maidi Feist-Belmont at a concert given by one of his friends, the singer Leo Slezak. Maidi, who was now Mrs. von Liebermann, had made Thoma's acquaintance earlier, in 1904. Now his affection for her was suddenly and strongly revived. He was overjoyed to learn from her that she was not happy in her marriage and was contemplating a divorce. Thoma, realizing that he had been in love with her during the almost fourteen years that had passed since their parting, naturally encouraged her in these plans. He wanted to do anything in his power in order to win this woman he had once lost. From 1918 until Thoma's death, countless letters traveled between them. Maidi became his new hope, and he looked forward with greatest joy to seeing her as often as possible. In November 1918 he traveled to Berlin in the midst of the turmoil of a revolution in order to visit Maidi. There he saw the orderly capital transformed into an apocalyptic stage for shooting, street battles, and mob rule. To Josef Hofmiller, he wrote: "Let Berlin go to the devil and everything with it that poisoned our Germany, and which has brought about her fate by arrogant and undutiful actions."[41]

The deepest crisis of Thoma's life set in after the defeat of Germany. He saw a world disappear which he had loved dearly, despite all of its shortcomings. This world had made him what he was, after all. In it was founded the meaning of his works. How should it now all perish? His old feelings of guilt began to intensify.

In these dark hours, Maidi emerged as the bright star on Thoma's horizon. Although he was already fifty years old, he saw the realization of his dream of a happy family life still within reach. He regretted the time lost to Marion that could have been spent most beautifully with Maidi at his side. In a letter to Conrad Haussmann, Thoma writes: "No man has ever spoiled happiness more for himself than I did."[42]

During the confusing months after the end of the war, Thoma felt an obligation to involve himself, at least indirectly, in Germany's politics. The November Revolution in Berlin, the Communist agitation all over Germany, the establishment of the Free State of Bavaria, the peace conference in Versailles and its ominous treaty agreements, the deplorable weakness of the Weimar Republic, the increasing poverty in Germany—all these events forced Thoma to, as he thought, help Germany by alerting its people to the evil forces inside and outside the country. His decision not to remain silent in the face of chaos and decay led to his involvement in a journalistic campaign against the political left. The *Miesbacher Anzeiger*, a local newspaper published in Miesbach, a district town

situated approximately ten miles east of Tegernsee, became the
public organ through which Thoma launched his attacks against the
enemies of Germany. The little paper's circulation, ridiculously
small at the beginning, jumped to very high figures after Thoma
began publishing his articles in it anonymously. The controversial
publisher of the *Anzeiger* was Klaus Eck, a man who had become
involved in countless lawsuits because of the belligerent character
of the statements and opinions expressed in his paper. Eck was obviously most interested in contributions from a figure of public esteem, as Ludwig Thoma was. Many of the one hundred and forty-
nine articles which Thoma wrote for the *Anzeiger* Eck picked up
himself at Thoma's house. Others were sent to an accommodation
address in Miesbach. Thoma's contributions to the *Miesbacher
Anzeiger* were written during 1919, 1920, and early 1921. For the
last time in his life, these articles, although written on highly controversial subjects, show the spontaneous and powerful fighter
Thoma could become as soon as he identified with an idea which
seemed worthy to him. They also reveal the fact that Thoma was
everything but a diplomatic or cautious politician. At least in part,
he was a coarse Bavarian who often had to suppress his overwhelming desire for a wild brawl, such as are still being fought with fists
and mugs every weekend in Bavaria's beer halls, taverns, and
restaurants.

Thoma's temper, which had been boiling for a long time, needed
this eruption in the old-Bavarian manner. He felt his ambition and
the old fire of his youth return. To Maidi he wrote: "There is an
ability to work in me, as never before. Within this year I could write
a number of novels."[43] And later he continues: "I [always] was and
I am [now] a man who forever stood up against repression and one
who never wants to keep quiet. When they . . . beat around the
bush in futility, I shall . . . beat the heads of this bunch of swine
until they lose hearing and sight."[44] It has to be kept in mind that
every one of the articles written for the *Miesbacher Anzeiger*
represents a pamphlet against the new rulers of Germany and the
powers of the *entente*. Thoma received no honorarium. It was pure
idealism and his anger about the lost war and the hopelessness of
the situation which drove him to write the articles. At the same
time, Thoma knew that he was not a born politician, nor did he ever
have the desire to be one. His own words express this best:

At the time when I wrote the *Vöst* [*Andreas Vöst*], the *Zentrum* [Center
party] was in power, [and the power it had,] . . . it abused recklessly. To-

day the *Sozialdemokratie* [Social Democratic party] is master, and it does even worse things. To fight the *Zentrum* today would mean to violate a corpse, but one has to stand up vigorously against the disgusting doctrinaires who are ruining our country. I have never had any joy [in talking politics]. I shall express my opinon as I always did. In this matter I have never missed an opportunity. I have to accomplish positive things, I have to work. There is nothing to be accomplished in criticizing, in making speeches and in talking politics. That is all sterile. With every new day, I better understand Goethe, who also hated this useless way of life.[45]

One of Thoma's idols throughout his life, Goethe increasingly became a reference point and a source of wisdom during his last years. In Thoma's correspondence with Maidi one finds quite a number of references to Goethe and his works. Thoma felt a great urge to share with the woman he loved the practical wisdom he found in the life and actions of the great Weimar master.

The other lodestar of Thoma's last few years was Bismarck. To Maidi Thoma wrote in November 1918 that he was planning to write a drama about the Iron Chancellor.[46] In another letter, he affirms these intentions.[47] Unfortunately, he did not live to realize them. One year after World War I had ended, he wrote: "Bismarck's letters—yes, in them is all of Germany, and everything which is magnificent in it."[48] In his last reference to Bismarck, he scolds the behavior of the "democrats" vis-à-vis the chancellor, remembering the disgraceful way in which he was dismissed:

On March 20, 1890, Bismarck left, accompanied by the triumphant howls of the democrats, of the *Sozis* and of the *Zentrum*. All these great politicians were glad that the leader was taken away from the Empire, and they did not see that everything which then followed had to happen the way it did when the ingrateful babbler [the emperor] acted as chancellor himself. In the whole Parliament there was no one who had recognized the danger, and no one who possessed the tact to protect the founder of the German Empire as a necessary consultant against the pliable Wilhelm. On April 1, 1895, the Parliament refused to congratulate Prince Bismarck on his eightieth birthday. These fools were not able to force the emperor back to reason.[49]

More than ever before, Thoma saw the fall of Bismarck as the beginning of the German catastrophe.

The year 1920 was again marked by a severe loss. Thoma's closest friend of the past five years, Ludwig Ganghofer, died suddenly in July at the age of sixty-five. Thoma accompanied his dead friend during his last journey across the Tegernsee to the graveyard in Egern. Only a week before, the two had been together at

Ganghofer's house, talking about hunting and about Thoma's new hunting story which he was in the process of writing. It later appeared under the title *Jagerloisl*. Now Ganghofer was resting by the churchyard wall. At the funeral, Thoma decided to buy the adjacent lot for his own grave, not knowing that within a few months he would have to join his friend there.

Only intensive work prevented Thoma from constant mourning. After finishing *Jagerloisl* in a remarkably short time, he began to draft plans for *Kaspar Lorinser*, and autobiographical novel in the style of Gottfried Keller's *Der grüne Heinrich*. Death prevented Thoma from finishing this novel.

During his work on *Kaspar Lorinser*, Thoma was increasingly plagued by concerns and sorrows of various kinds. The decay of Germany under the new regime seemed to continue at an increasing pace. The symptoms were the insecurity, the vanishing of traditions, and the growing radicalism of the postwar years. It is not surprising that Thoma feared for the survival of his work. Although the term of copyright extended to thirty years after publication, he was uncertain whether he, or in the case of his death, Maidi, could rely on a steady income from royalties. He suspected that the changing political climate which clearly indicated a dangerous leap to the left could turn people away from his books, which were, after all, written for people who loved their homeland and its traditions. During long conversations, he shared his apprehensions about the fate of Germany with Josef Hofmiller. One is tempted to compare Thoma's expressions of concern about the new, evil world with those of the medieval poets Walther von der Vogelweide and Neidhart von Reuenthal at the end of their lives.

Contributing to Thoma's gloomy outlook on the world was Maidi's hesitation to entirely break with her husband and join Thoma at the "Tuften." His hopes for a marriage began to dwindle, and loneliness and bad temper increasingly burdened his solitary life. Finally he told Maidi:

[For me to come] for two days to Heidelberg, particularly with Mama and Bubi there, and in this sad, depressed mood . . . would be a torture for you and me. I cannot cut my heart out of my body and be thoughtless and gay. If others can do this, I am unable to. I am not harsh, Maidi, and I do what I can to show you that I love you. Are you doing [the same]? At Easter, you said so firmly that you wanted to come here [to the "Tuften"] at Pentecost. Now Heidelberg is the word . . . to have Bubi and Mama with you. . . . Do you think it is beautiful to sit here completely alone, to see the spring and feel what I feel? If it is more important to be in Kümmelbach with Bubi, or to show me that I do not stand entirely alone and that I still have a task yet, that you must know. To go on trips! And to know that Germans are being shot down like dogs without a master at the same hour. To enjoy things! And to be frightened by one's own self when one laughs.

You two, you and Mama, you take as a strange mood that which is [really] nothing but anger and pain, as I see the dearest [thing] in this world, the old German fatherland, being destroyed. Why don't we understand each other in this? I do not know why, but I cannot change it. . . .[50]

This letter represents the most direct and desperate expression of discouragement and grief Thoma sent to Maidi. On the night of Ludwig Ganghofer's death, his wife had said to Thoma that he should not wait too long to take Maidi to the "Tuften," because life is so short. Since then, the thought that his love was living her own life far away and among strange people became increasingly unbearable for him. Maidi had to take the step which had been overdue for such a long time.

Another letter to Maidi, similar in content, but a little milder in tone, followed on the next day. For the first time, Thoma mentioned something about being ill.[51] For quite some time, he had felt a strange pressure in his stomach which kept him awake during the night and which took away his appetite. He had never fully recovered from the dysentery which he had brought home from the Eastern Front. The photographs we have of Thoma from the time after 1916 indeed show a steady decline in his appearance, particularly in his face. Friends who visited him sometimes found him worn and of an almost gray complexion.

Work was the only device for Thoma to forget his lingering ailment and the constant, nagging pain. During these days in early summer of 1921, he finished his collection of essays entitled *Leute, die ich kannte*. All through spring he had worked very intensively on a peasant novel with a tragic ending which he called *Der Ruepp*. At the end of July 1921 the pains in his stomach must have become intolerable. He decided to undergo a thorough checkup at the Red Cross Hospital in Munich. Professor Stubenrauch, a well-known surgeon, advised him that an operation would be necessary immediately. Dr. Stubenrauch's diagnosis indicated that Thoma was suffering from a hernia complicated by the fact that stomach and diaphragm were grown together. In the early morning of August 5, 1921, Thoma entered the hospital. A few hours later, already in his hospital room, he wrote to Maidi: "Boehm [the surgeon] calls the operation an almost everyday affair, and the nurses also seem to be informed the same way. At least one of them said, 'Oh, that is indeed a simple matter,' when I gave my name at the check-in.—Now I sit alone in my room, hearing factory whistles, moving streetcars, nothing else, and I am thinking only about you, and I hope and wish, you dear, good girl, that you are as calm as I am. All dear and good thoughts are with you, you sweet girl. When you will have this letter in your hands, the matter will be already settled. So long, so long!"[52] It was the last letter to Maidi von Liebermann.

On the morning of the next day, Professor Stubenrauch and Professor Boehm performed the surgery. As it turned out, the cancer of the stomach, from which the patient had been suffering, was already too far advanced. Without knowing about his malignant disease, Thoma spent fourteen days after the operation in the Red Cross Hospital. On August 20, 1921, he requested that he be transported home to the "Tuften," where he was hoping to speed up his obviously slow recovery, under the care of his two sisters.

He arrived in Rottach on August 24, and the next day, on August 25, 1921, he wrote his last letter, which was addressed to Prince G. von Donnersmarck: "At home! Yesterday I came here in an automobile, and, although it was quite an effort, the gain was great. Everything is different here. I am under the most meticulous care, in wonderful air. I enjoy every noise in here and outside the house, and I hear, feel, breathe home. In the newspaper there was a foolish note saying that I suffered from critical weakness of the heart; I did not suffer from it at any time. Always normal. Only the stomach has to be fed carefully.—For your magnificent gentians and Ritter's work, I say my sincerest thanks to you. It was a great, dear, All Saints' Day joy.—And now I send you a dear greeting from home."[53]

In the evening of the next day, Thoma died. He had been hopeful about his recovery until the very end, not knowing the severity of his ailment.

Many people accompanied the dead poet to his last resting place, in the churchyard in Egern, including Duke Ludwig Wilhelm of Bavaria, Professor Boehm, Maidi von Liebermann, the singer Leo Slezak, Conrad Haussmann (who delivered the funeral oration), the mountaineer rifle company of Tegernsee, representatives of various societies, forest rangers from Tegernsee and from far away, and countless farmers.

Ludwig Thoma is buried beside his friend Ludwig Ganghofer, whom he survived by only a few months.

CHAPTER 2

Plays

I Die Medaille (*The Medal*) *Comedy in One Act*

DISTRICT Supervisor Heinrich Kranzeder has decided to give a festive dinner in honor of his office clerk, Peter Neusigl, who has served the Bavarian Crown for fifty years, and who will, at this occasion, receive the Silver Medal of Merit. Kranzeder's wife, Amalie, who takes exception to the fact that her parlor is to be used to entertain people of such inferior social standing, is told by her husband that the real purpose for giving the dinner is to impress his superior, Director Steinbeissel, who has also been invited in order that he may witness Kranzeder's popularity among the dignitaries of his district, most of whom are, in fact, rather simple people, even though some of them hold political office. Lampl, a butcher, is the local representative in the State Diet; Merkl and Grubhofer, two farmers, are members of the District Committee; Hahnrieder and Sedlmaier are farmers from the area; and Häberlein is the local schoolteacher. Assessor von Hingerl, Kranzeder's assistant, also takes part in the festivity. He has been instructed to propose a toast to the district office during the course of the dinner.

Shortly after the dinner has started, tension between Kranzeder and his wife, and von Hingerl, on the one side, and the guests, on the other side, begins to surface. Although Kranzeder tries repeatedly to guide the dinner conversation by asking questions about current political issues in the district, such as the tax structure, the building of a new railroad, etc., he is not successful in pacifying the increasingly agitated participants in the disputes. Before long the farmers begin to disagree on issues even among themselves. Merkl and Grubhofer, who are in serious disagreement over the funding of a new district road in the area, almost start a fistfight. Only a toast in honor of Neusigl and his wife interrupts their quarrel.

74

Witnessing the deteriorating atmosphere at the dinner table and the increasingly uninhibited behavior of Häberlein, who is not used to drinking wine, Kranzeder nervously awaits the arrival of Director Steinbeissel, which is mysteriously delayed. Finally, Häberlein, already heavily drunk, proposes a toast to the lady of the house. Babbling and stuttering in his stupor, he praises Amalie Kranzeder for being a living example of the proverb: "Youth vanishes, but virtue endures." No longer able to suffer the inappropriate behavior of the guests, Kranzeder and his wife jump up from their seats. While Kranzeder is shouting that he cannot tolerate this debauchery any longer, and Amalie is calling Häberlein's toast an infamy, Grubhofer and Merkl take the tumultuous moment as the opportunity to get at each other's throats, a chance they have been waiting for all evening. In the course of the ensuing brawl, the dinner table crashes to the floor. Amalie Kranzeder furiously blames her husband for the catastrophic evening, and just as she is about to storm out of the room on von Hingerl's arm, Director Steinbeissel makes his long-awaited entrance. When the severe-looking director sees the fighting and the table turned upside down, he demands an explanation from the stupefied and deadly embarrassed Kranzeder. Stuttering sheepishly, Kranzeder tries to explain that he had intended to celebrate the bestowal of the Medal of Merit in an accordingly appropriate festivity. The play ends with the director's highly suggestive comment: "Is that so?"

Die Medaille was Thoma's first success as a stage author. After he had finished the play in the fall of 1900, the director of the Munich *Hoftheater*, Ernst von Possart, accepted it for production. The stage director Jocza Savits, who had turned down Thoma's first play, *Witwen*, was rather pleasantly surprised by his old friend's new work. The first performance of *Medaille* took place on August 24, 1901, as part of a double billing with the dramatic farce *Der Hochzeitstag*, by Wilhelm Wolters. It was Thoma's play, however, that made the evening. One can imagine how happy the author was. In a letter of August 28, 1901, addressed to his mentor, Albert Langen, he expressed his pride:

My first performance here went over so well that it was beyond expectation. "Stormy success" the *Neueste [Nachrichten]* commented, but two days later they found that (this) kind of rudeness did not entirely fit the stage of the *Hoftheater*. The social-democratic *Post* was overcome by joy and called me the "great laugher," etc. This kind of praise could hurt me here [in

Munich], because the ultramontane papers picked up the play and found it "unheard of" that Possart had accepted the *Medaille* [for performance]. The *Münchner Tagblatt* wrote that he [Possart] should invite the Chamber [of deputies], which would soon be in session, to this mockery. —It may well be that the issue will be talked about in the Chamber and that Possart will get scared. But perhaps Possart will remain firm when he sees how well things are going. —Yesterday's sold-out performance was an even stronger laughing success than the first performance.—But, as I said, perhaps he is still afraid of the deputies.[1]

Possart did not get scared by the deputies. He stuck to his newest stage author, whose subsequent plays were to become an important part of the theater's standard repertoire and would be the most frequently performed plays at the Munich *Hoftheater* for several decades.

The initial success of *Die Medaille* was by no means only a local one. On October 28, 1901, Ernst von Wolzogen opened his new stage, the *Überbrettl*, on Berlin's Köpenickstrasse with a performance of the play. Soon afterwards other theaters, such as those in Hamburg, Stuttgart, Nuremberg, and even in the stage metropolis, Vienna, followed suit.

Why was *Die Medaille* such an overwhelming success? The answer is obvious to the reader of the play: all the mistakes which Thoma had made in *Witwen*, his first, unsuccessful comedy, he avoids in the new play. He never gets overwhelmed by the milieu, but keeps a healthy balance between the strong characters and the small district town atmosphere which serves as background for the plot. Although the two elements never clash with each other, as they do in *Witwen*, the author now distinctly favors portraying the figures in a realistic manner. There is no paleness or shallowness, no idealizing. The people on the stage are real and totally credible. There is the district supervisor, a cheap opportunist, who uses the sanctum of his parlor for the celebration of his office clerk's service anniversary, in itself an unnecessary, even ridiculous exercise. He pays dearly for his hypocrisy and zeal. He has to fight a two-front war between the "primitive and uneducated" farmers and his bigoted, Lyceum-educated wife, who despises her simple guests, whom she regards as intruders, and who considers herself a person who would rather associate with nobility and high government officials. The assistant's (Assessor von Hingerl's) personality brilliantly complements that of the wife of the district supervisor. He is totally above associating with common people and is unable or unwilling to understand their way of living, working, thinking, or enjoying themselves.

It is the clash of social spheres at the end of the nineteenth century on which Thoma bases much of the substance of *Die Medaille*. For several reasons, it was indeed impossible for the simple and the "elevated" people—meaning the lower and upper-middle classes—to communicate with each other. First of all, there were century-old social borders fully intact within the Germany society, with accompanying traditional feelings of mutual distrust and contempt between farmers and urban people. These very profound antagonisms have not been totally erased in our time; they have diminished at best. And they are by no means limited to Germany or Central Europe, but are apparent within all modern societies. The second element, the animosity between "Arch-Bavarians" and "non-Arch-Bavarians," which is specifically tied to the sociological situation of Bavaria in the late nineteenth and early twentieth centuries, enhances the hostile feelings on both sides. It has a long history. Without going back too far, one can detect its first outbreak at the time of Napoleon's occupation of Germany and during the period immediately following. For political reasons the French emperor had favored Bavaria by a significant enlargement of its territory, incorporating areas of Württemberg in the west and Franconia in the north, thereby forming a new kingdom, whereas up to then Bavaria had only held the rank of an electorate within the Holy Roman Empire. After Napoleon's fall, the Wittelsbach dynasty, then reigning in Bavaria, began to attract scholars and artists, mainly from the North of Germany, to Munich, their new capital, in an effort to make it into a cultural metropolis equal to Paris and Vienna. Emulating Napoleon's concept of a strong central administration, the Wittelsbachers also created a large and complicated bureaucracy largely composed of individuals from the Franconian part of the new state. This "foreign" influx into the Bavarian civil service increased following the unification of Germany after the Franco-German War of 1870 - 71, when a large number of Prussian administrators began to infiltrate various levels of public service. It should be noted that this new development was even less welcomed by the native population of "Old Bavarians" than the wave of Franconian immigration to Munich. These new, and often rather young, officials of Prussian extraction were met with deep antipathy, and even contempt. In part, this attitude of the natives toward the newcomers may be explained as a means of repaying the arrogance with which the Bavarians were treated by their "Prussian brothers," who enjoyed looking down on the "outmoded" Bavarian ways, and who considered the Bavarian people to be as backwards and artless as their "strange" dialect with its archaic phonology. Additionally, the belief in limitless industrialization and in the rapid enlargement of urban areas held by the Prussian administrators stood in sharp contrast to the conservative convictions of the rural population. These profound differences and all the ensuing misunderstandings appeared unbridgeable in Thoma's time, as they do even today. Assessor von Hingerl, like many other Thoma characters, is a vivid example of "Prussianism" in Bavaria.

If, in his lofty, snobbish bearing, the assessor may be said to represent the extreme on the Prussian side, Grubhofer and Merkl are fine specimens of the Bavarian way of doing things. They settle their dispute in an old-fashioned fistfight, with no regard to where they are, or with whom. In refusing to accept any offer of mediation, they display a stubbornness that is a typical and dominant trait in the Bavarian farmer's character. Although this subject will be touched upon later, it should be noted that the word "forgiveness" seems to be almost foreign to the vocabulary of the Bavarian farmer, as if Christianity, and the New Testament, otherwise so important in the life of these farmers, had left the underlying ancient, pagan code of ethics untouched. Grubhofer's and Merkl's way of settling a dispute by physical means is rather characteristic for vast areas of rural South Germany and indicative of a traditional longing for a good scuffle. Weekend fights on a large scale and often resulting in extensive property damage still occur more or less regularly in most regions of Upper and Lower Bavaria.

Lampl, Hahnrieder, and Sedlmaier represent the voice of moderation. Their table manners do not resemble those of the educated cityfolks, but they are certainly more refined than Grubhofer or Merkl. They are members of the local political machine, and Lampl has even served as a deputy to the national assembly in Berlin. They all know how to deal with the "educated class": always appear humble in the beginning, but show them at the right time that you know your worth and are capable of defending yourself. Sometimes, when the situation allows, quickly humiliate the other party by letting him know that his booklearning would not solve any of the farmers' problems.

Häberlein represents a very special type among the comic figures of the play. He is a schoolteacher and, unbeknownst to him, his dilemma is that he belongs to neither of the factions described above. He is certainly no farmer, nor does he belong to the privileged class of bureaucrats. He stands right in the middle. His education and position elevate him above the general populace only so long as he moves in his professional milieu. As far as his economic status is concerned, he ranks very low among the dinner guests. As Lampl emphasizes, Häberlein would never miss a free meal. He is also the only one at the table who overindulges in the consumption of wine, thereby indirectly helping to create the mood which leads to the final brawl. By reciting his little aphorisms at every possible (inopportune) occasion, he is trying to show his superior level of education, which is also reflected in his High German pronunciation. Häberlein is a member of the then-unfortunate class of grade-school teachers who were underpaid and notoriously ridiculed for their relative indigence and eccentricity.

Finally, there are the guests of honor: Peter Neusigl and his wife, Walburga. They are perfect examples of an honorable, petit-bourgeois couple, as they existed by the millions in the nineteenth century. Peter Neusigl is a very steady, loyal, and hard worker, reliable and honest. There is no false modesty in him or in his wife: when he tells about the emergencies he and his boss have had to attend to over the years, he mentions himself first, and Kranzeder only incidentally.[2] When he praises Kranzeder, one gets the impression that he really regards his boss as the best district supervisor who ever served under him (Neusigl), and not vice versa. He is convinced that he and his immense administrative experience are totally indispensable for the district. His wife underscores his opinion in her conversation with the other guests, stating repeatedly that her husband is much too modest. The exaggeration of her husband's talents reaches a peak when she tells Kranzeder that Peter's brother, who is also a minor government worker, always told her that Peter should not have become a lawyer (which, of course, he is not), but that he should have gone into medicine, where he could have advanced much further. One can imagine how Kranzeder receives such a well-intended statement from his clerk's wife. Speaking in an affected mixture of colloquial and High German, she is also successful in antagonizing Amalie Kranzeder, who is repelled by her repeated attempts to strike up a conversation with her. When Amalie learns that the Neusigls keep a domestic servant, she cannot hide her amazement about "these people's standard of undeserved luxury."[3] Conversing with the assessor, she points out "these people's" expensive eating habits when she hears Mrs. Neusigl continuously talk about fried meat dishes.[4]

What were Thoma's intentions in writing his first successful stage play? First, and most importantly, he wanted to make both the viewer and the reader laugh wholeheartedly. He wanted Die Medaille to be a truly funny comedy, not a didactic play, although didactic elements are not entirely lacking. He succeeded brilliantly. Die Medaille has become a German classic. The play also serves as a monument to the figure of the overzealous, servile bureaucrat and his limitless opportunism. The opportunist receives just punishment for his hypocrisy: the country people, on whom he had always looked down, but whom he would use for his selfish purpose, turn his dinner party into a brawl before the eyes of his much-feared superior, who was supposed to have been impressed by the district supervisor's great popularity among the people of the district. In short, with Die Medaille, Thoma had discovered the literary field which would grow his best products, namely those of realistic comedy.

II   Die Lokalbahn *(The Branch Line)*
Comedy in Three Acts

Friedrich Rehbein, burgomaster of Dornstein, a medium-sized rural Bavarian town, returns from Munich, where he has had an appointment with the transportation minister concerning the alignment of a projected branch line (*Lokalbahn*), which would connect the town with the general railway system. The government wants to put the projected terminal one quarter of an hour away from town instead of in it. The purpose of the burgomaster's unsuccessful visit with the minister was to change the government's stance on the issue. When at his return he is met by his family and several citizens of Dornstein, who are anxious to hear about the outcome of his conference, he tells them that he has not been able to change the minister's mind. He hints that he had nevertheless told him off, giving him his opinion about the shabby way the Dornsteiners had been dealt with by the government, and leaving the startled minister in a totally perplexed state. Proud of their burgomaster's courage, the Dornstein citizens have their choral society give him a serenade. Enjoying his undeserved triumph, the burgomaster begins to believe his own story about his clash with the minister. On the next morning he has to bear the consequences of his ac-

tion: his daughter Susanna's fiancé, a junior judge at the district
court, by the name of Beringer, is upset by an article in the local
paper praising the burgomaster's courage in standing up against the
government. He arrives to announce that the engagement is off. His
career would be in grave danger were his supervisors to learn that
he was about to marry the daughter of a burgomaster with
revolutionary ambitions.

Realizing the trouble his exaggerations are causing his family, the
burgomaster tells his brother, a retired army major, the true story of
his visit: the minister had behaved like friendliness personified, and
to a friendly person one cannot be rude. On his return to Dornstein,
he just could not tell his citizens that he had taken the whole matter
lying down. Now his family has to pay for his false pride.

With the truth finally told, the burgomaster begins repairing the
damage: when a delegation of town councilmen voice their concern
that the newspaper article would also be read in Munich and be interpreted as an act of insubordination, Rehbein explains that he has
already decided to travel to Munich to apologize to the minister.
The burgomaster is again congratulated for his courage. He then
confesses to Beringer that there was no truth to his account and that
he would personally express his indignation about the newspaper
article to the minister. Moderately pleased, Beringer decides not to
break the engagement after all.

Rehbein and his family celebrate the newly won peace in the
family and among the citizens of Dornstein with a glass of beer. To
his surprise the choral society again arrives, followed by a large
number of citizens. This time they praise the burgomaster's self-
control, which permits them to remain in the good graces of the
government.

Thoma began to write *Die Lokalbahn* during his stay in Berlin in
1902. On October 19, 1902, the play directed by Jocza Savits, had
its first performance at the Munich *Hoftheater*. The performance
was a full success, although Thoma, who observed the acting from
behind the curtain, recognized that minor changes in the dialogue
would be necessary. In a letter to Albert Langen on October 21,
1902, he makes some critical comments:

I have learned a lot during the rehearsals and during the first performance,
and I hope to be able to benefit from my experience. The mood among the
audience after the first and the second act was better than I had expected. . . . The public called me before the curtain already after the first

act. But I only went out after the second and third act. . . . The house was
sold out, and it is again today. . . . The people laughed a great deal, [and]
several times there was applause during the opening scenes. . . . Madame
Ramlo, as Mrs. Pilgermaier, was wonderful. Mr. Suske, as the burgomaster,
was a little bit North German, but very good. Perhaps you shall see the
Lokalbahn yourself in the not-too-distant future. . . .[5]

A few days later, in another letter to Langen dated November 6,
1902, after more reviews had appeared, Thoma talks about his position vis-à-vis the critics in the serene manner he had already
adapted at the time of the *Medaille* success, and gives a further ex-
plication of the play:

I am as apathetic toward the reviewers of *Die Lokalbahn* as usual. Every
critic has either written an unsuccessful play himself, or he is about to write
one. What do I care about the opinion of a *Schnorralist* [Thoma's own funny version of "Journalist"]. . . . I know that I am ill-liked by the literati.
But that cannot be avoided if one is the editor of the *Simplicissimus*. . . .
Whoever wants to see a theatrical farce in *Lokalbahn* can do that if he
wants to, but the important thing is that it is far from being one. . . . I
know that the first and second act are without fault, and that they contain
not one scene which appears to be "farfetched." The third act leaves
something to be desired. For the theater's sake, I should have put in more
"spectacle.". . . Aside from all that, it is pleasant, as far as the financial
point is concerned. Were it not for that, I would never write a play again;
artistically, it does not interest me nearly as much as the most simple
Novelle. One suffers pain when one sees one's play being performed even
in the best manner. All the atmosphere vanishes, every milieu becomes
rude and crude in the limelight.[6]

A very self-confident author speaks through these lines, a
playwright no critic could impress with his biting reviews. *Die
Lokalbahn* was only the second among Thoma's successful comedies. Nevertheless, he already saw himself as a seasoned
playwright. Even if one considers that this letter was addressed to
Albert Langen, who undoubtedly savored Thoma's spicy words and
hearty expressions, the writer's blasé mood is apparent.

The best of his comedies, *Erster Klasse*, was yet to come, but after
Die Lokalbahn Thoma had already grown a little tired of writing
plays. There were some external reasons for this, of course. "Old
Viktor" had died shortly after the first performance of *Die
Lokalbahn*,[7] and her sudden death had spelled the end of the
Vorderriss world. It was not only that "old Viktor" could no longer

share in his joy and happiness; almost all of the people who had meant something to Thoma were gone. On the eve of the performance of *Die Lokalbahn* at the Vienna *Burgtheater*, Thoma felt deeply that all the honors this world could bestow now meant very little. His mother and many beloved friends were dead, and they were the ones who would have most enjoyed his triumph.[8]

Die Lokalbahn differs significantly from *Die Medaille*, where the dialogue occupies a very dominant position. In the earlier play, the course of the action depended largely on the discussion developing at the dinner table, when one word leads to the next. The action of *Die Lokalbahn* gravitates around one event, the burgomaster's return from an important conference with the minister, which could have changed the fate of the whole town. Every citizen is curious and expects good news. The burgomaster cannot give them the desired news because that would constitute an outright lie. But he cannot resist the temptation to appear as a Spartan hero who has fought an invincible government and has been defeated. Again, the characters are carefully drawn, and appear remarkably realistic. The burgomaster of Dornstein (which, in all probability, stands for "Traunstein") is a reasonably educated man, well-liked by the state government and very popular with the citizens. A likeable person and a good diplomat, he is somewhat opportunistic. He has great respect for his brother, the retired army major, who is certainly free of any opportunism and represents the burgomaster's conscience, his honest side, so to speak. However, when the burgomaster sees his reputation fade and his family in disarray, he secretly blames his brother's sarcasm, and his own fear of it, for his own foolish swindle. Although he enjoys the citizens' ovation, he begins to tremble when he recognizes the consequences of his deception for his family. The major, on the other hand, is an entirely different man. He likes clear-cut solutions. When he discusses the railroad issue, he lets everybody (including Beringer) know that he would find it natural for his brother to protest against the arbitrary decision of the government, particularly since it is based on the selfish desire of a nobleman-industrialist who wants the rail connection for his brick works. The major has a very sound feeling for justice and is always ready to defend it, regardless of cost. He represents the old-style military officer, duty-conscious and always prepared to wage a war against indecency. When it is learned that Beringer has broken the engagement with Susanna, the major is the only one who welcomes the development. For him, it is preferable that the opportunistic character of Beringer is discovered before the marriage. He takes Beringer for someone who is incapable of any real feelings, but who coldly breaks with Susanna the moment he sees his career endangered by the alleged protest actions of her father. When he later learns that nothing is at stake, he returns to Susanna, once again showing no emotion. The most despicable figure in the whole play, Beringer is an egocentric, spineless lad with nothing in mind but his court cases, over which he frequently broods, and his advancement within the hierarchy of civil service.

Beringer has a somewhat less abominable counterpart among the female cast of the play in the character of Mrs. Rehbein, Susanna's mother. She is very apprehensive about her husband's trip to the capital, to protest against the minister's decision, since by so doing he might blemish his excellent record and lose his good standing with the minister, in addition to spoiling his chances of becoming a deputy in the assembly. When Susanna's happiness is threatened, she puts everything on the line. After the truth is known, she rushes to Beringer and explains to him that all the talk about her husband's courage in defending the Dornsteiners' position and about the harsh words he had used against the minister was fabricated.

The one figure in the play who best understands the motives behind Mrs. Rehbein's actions is brewer Schweigel, who is a good family man himself. After his anger at the national railroads over the loss of his vegetable garden, through which the proposed branch line would pass, has subsided, he realizes that nothing is more important than to live in peace with the government and to have a peaceful home. In this conviction, he represents the majority of the Dornstein citizens, who in the brief adventure of a glorious fight had forgotten these important principles. When the major tries to make an issue over the brewer's inconsistency during the events of the previous two days, the latter sums up his feelings in a few words: "You have to understand me right. I say, myself, that steadfastness is something beautiful. Morally speaking, I am in agreement with you, but the other view also has its justification."[9]

It is "the other view," the one of expedience and convenience, which remains victorious in *Die Lokalbahn*. Even the major, who is the most honorable character in the play, can do little about that. In his dispute with his sister-in-law, he gives in and promises to play the game according to her (and, as it turns out, everybody else's) rules in the future, but not without reminding her, at the same time, that she is wrong.

Die Lokalbahn gives the viewer and reader a lot to think about as a portrait of real life as it exists, and not only in small towns. And, who is the real winner in the end? Apparently, the government and its railroad. For their own purposes, however, the citizens of Dornstein also celebrate a victory, because they have overcome their inclination to doubt, and even contradict, the infinite wisdom of the minister. In their burgomaster, they have a representative worthy of their thinking.

III   Moral *(Morals) Comedy in Three Acts*

The head of the Moral Society, Rentier Beermann, is a wealthy bourgeois in his best years and an important person in his town of Emilsburg, the capital of the dukedom of Gerolstein. He is planning to run for a seat in the National Assembly. While entertaining several notable citizens in his lavishly decorated apartment, among them several members of the Moral Society, including Professor Wasner and Mr. Bolland, the owner of a soap factory, he learns about the arrest of a certain Ninon de Hauteville, a lady of the town who led an all-too-active social life, and who is supposed to have favored the intimate association of a number of gentlemen in important positions.

The young and zealous Assessor Ströbel has taken charge of the case. Although he is cautioned by the police chief not to cause any embarrassment to people in high places, he is determined to get to the bottom of the affair. Already in possession of Hauteville's diary, he decides to interrogate her. She refuses to cooperate. The identity of certain persons who hid in her wardrobe during the police raid cannot be forced out of her.

Beermann is extremely worried since he and some of his friends have been among the frequent visitors to Hauteville's apartment. Fearing for their reputations, he steals Hauteville's diary from police headquarters while Ströbel is distracted by a phone call announcing the arrival of Baron von Schmettau, adjutant of his Highness the Prince of Gerolstein. Beermann slips out of Ströbel's office and does not hear Baron von Schmettau reveal that the two persons forced to hide in Hauteville's wardrobe were none other than his Highness the prince and himself, the Baron, who demands that the case against Hauteville be dismissed immediately and with utmost discretion. After apologizing for the clumsy way the police behaved during the raid, the police chief blames Ströbel for the em-

barrassing situation and promises that Hauteville will be released
that same evening. Ströbel will take care of the details.

At his apartment, Beermann is disclosing his involvement in the
affair and his theft of the diary to his friend, Dr. Hauser, a government lawyer, when they are interrupted by the unexpected arrival
of Professor Wasner, who has come to confess that it was he, a
dutiful member of the Moral Society, who tipped off the police
about the immoral activities of Madame Hauteville, after he himself
had fallen victim to her wicked charm.

As the involvement of more and more members of the Moral
Society becomes apparent, a meeting is called to deal with the problem of containing the widening scandal. Ströbel, who has been
charged with discreetly settling the matter, informs Beermann of
Hauteville's demand for ten.thousand marks in return for quietly
leaving town. Should the police not agree to her conditions, she will
insist on a trial. Von Schmettau urges Beermann, as head of the
Moral Society, to immediately find a solution to the problem of
silencing Hauteville, making it clear that his Highness will not contribute any funds.

An appropriate solution to the dilemma presents itself as Beermann decides to take up a collection from among the members of
the Moral Society. Theirs is the responsibility, after all, of safeguar-
ding the public morals. Greatly relieved, Baron von Schmettau con-
gratulates Beermann for his wise decision and promises him a high
decoration from the Duke.

Thoma's plans for *Moral* date back to his imprisonment in
Stadelheim during October and November of 1906, when he devis-
ed the plot and sketched most of the characters. After leaving
Stadelheim, other important matters, including planning and
building his stately home in Rottach, occupied his mind to the extent that he was unable to concentrate on the new play. And his
contributions to the *Simplicissimus*, as well as his work on the
Filserbriefe, demanded much time and effort. In May, 1908, the
house on the "Tuften" was completed, and he finally found his way
back to working on *Moral*, which was finished by early October.
Although *Moral* was to become one of Thoma's most successful
plays, writing it was not as easy as he would have liked. Some of his
letters written in 1908 suggest that he had become a little disgusted
with the plot. To Ganghofer he wrote: "For my part, I still sit
(working) on the comedy, filing and filing. Sometimes everything I
have done seems so boringly clever. Then it wanders into the

wastepaper basket, and of many pages only one line remains. It is difficult to say something new about a hackneyed theme."[10] And again in July: "I'll bring the comedy along, complete or three-fourths complete. But I want to hear your opinion. I know that you take great interest in it, and I thank you for that as cordially as you have written to me about it. This damned work is difficult. . . . I have to find always new thoughts, and I have to present the obvious in a new form. Sometimes I sweat profusely [over it]. For example, there is the conversation between the cocotte and the assessor. The model stands threatening in front of me, and I tear up one sheet of paper after another."[11] During August, nearing the completion of the play, he remarked: "I cannot afford to interrupt my work once more before it is completed in a rough form. . . . I have the last part of the second act in front of me; if I work without interruption, the third act can be finished in three weeks."[12]

Thoma finished the play on September 12, 1908. To Conrad Haussmann he wrote: "At this hour of midnight, I have just put the word 'end' under my comedy, *Moral*; then I gave a loud sigh, and after that watched the sky a little bit from the balcony. The stars do not show themselves tonight, and I cannot determine the child's nativity. . . . The theme was difficult, because it had been illuminated and discussed from every angle already. Now the play still has to face one great enemy: censorship."[13]

In spite of Thoma's skepticism, the play became an overwhelming success. The first performance took place on November 20, 1908, on the stage of the *Kleines Theater* in Berlin. Its director, Barnowsky, moved up the performance one day in order to get it on his stage before it could appear at the Munich *Schauspielhaus*, where the first performance was to have taken place originally. The Munich premiere, which followed on the twenty-first of November, was, nevertheless, still billed as "the first performance" on the printed announcement. I. G. Stollberg was the director there, and the famous actor Gustav Waldau played Baron von Schmettau. After the Munich premiere, there was great applause and it became obvious that the author's reservations had been unfounded. The play remained on the repertoire of several well-known theaters for an extended period of time, not only because Thoma already had an excellent reputation as a dramatist, but truly on its own merits. The play still survives on the stage. In 1930, it came out again in the Munich *Schauspielhaus* under the direction of Hans Schweikart, once more enjoying extreme popularity with the audience. In 1937, it was newly produced at the Munich *Prinzregententheater* under the direction of Peter Stanchina. Munich's *Residenztheater* produced *Moral* first in 1949, when Gerd Brüdern directed it, and then again in 1960 under the guidance of Helmut Heinrich. *Moral* has also been played many times in other major German cities, including Frankfurt am Main, where the legendary Heinrich George was among the cast; and in Berlin, where Ninon de Hauteville was played by Grete Weiser in a production at the *Volksbühne*.[14]

Although Thoma was initially apprehensive about the future of *Moral*, he was pleased about the principal motifs he had used in it. In a letter to Conrad Haussmann, he reveals a great deal about them: "Now I will present you with a few motifs. The first act I have left without strong action on purpose. First of all, I intended to describe opinions, but mainly I wanted to demonstrate that it is precisely an educated woman who can find arguments against hypocrisy and prudishness. . . . In the second and third act I wanted to heighten the tension, but at the same time I wanted to make it apparent—in spite of the fun involved—that the morals of our society are only of relative value. If you find that I was successful of keeping the development and the solution a surprise, that is all right with me. Now the child has to face the world and see for itself whether it can survive."[15]

An important factor contributing to the success of *Moral* was Thoma's consistent use of High German. Thus, the theatergoing public all over Germany was able to understand the lines of the play fully and instantaneously. This time it was very easy for Thoma to keep out dialect since the entire play deals with figures belonging to the wealthy bourgeoisie, the middle class and the nobility. Thoma had arrived at such a high level of dramatic characterization that he could refrain from using dialect without losing any comical substance.

Beermann, the main character, could carry the whole plot on his own. He is a perfect example of a petit bourgeois. While preaching the virtues of morality as president of the newly created Moral Society, he continues to pay regular visits to the town prostitute, naturally assuming that no one would find out about it, particularly not his wife. Principles are not his strong point: he is running for a seat in Parliament on a conservative-liberal platform, and therefore, in the words of Baron von Schmettau, is "truly not a doctrinaire."[16] When his wife reveals that she already knows about his dubious morals, he seems stunned but is certainly not permanently shocked.

In explaining his dilemma to his bachelor friend Hauser, he talks about his adventures as if they were a necessary part of any marriage. The same kind of reasoning surfaces in his conversation with Assessor Ströbel, also a bachelor, who has no interest in condoning the escapades of the "honorable" family men whose names are listed in the Hauteville diary. Beermann's appeal to Ströbel culminates in a reminder of the grave consequences the uncovering of a scandal of such proportions would entail: The masses would lose their respect for authority of any kind, and that could certainly not be in the interest of the police. Ströbel, the naive, young police official, believes in the absoluteness of the law, and he is not willing to listen to Beermann's arguments. Hauser, the sophisticated, seasoned lawyer, promises to help his friend, but not without ridiculing his highly questionable ethics. But any humiliation Beermann has to suffer during his conversation with Hauser leaves him ultimately undisturbed. He and his code of ethics seem to be rather indestructible.

Professor Wasner's morals, on the other hand, differ considerably from Beermann's. He feels guilty after having fallen "victim" to the lures of Ninon de Hauteville. But by his act of repentance he commits yet another ugly deed in tipping off the police, who he hopes will remove the source of his moral "fall" without his having to be exposed. He finds out too late that his own name is on the long list of "respectable" customers named in the diary. Now, Wasner, who has been the loudest voice for the cause of moral purity, is about to become a victim of his own hypocrisy and stupidity.

Wasner and Beermann have a more quiet counterpart in Bolland, who also turns out to be one of Hauteville's customers. He had never engaged in the preaching of morals, however, and shows himself to be the epitome of an uneducated, tasteless petit bourgeois, reckless and without sympathy for others, but not above soliciting it for himself. When he is in danger of being discovered as one of Hauteville's visitors, he suddenly becomes ill.

The remaining figures in the play do little to redeem the unvirtuous image which characterizes the males among the main characters. The police chief, a clever opportunist, delegates authority to his subordinate only in matters where he does not want to bear responsibility. In Ströbel he has found the perfect underling, a young, ambitious opportunist, almost drunk with his power as an interrogator. Ströbel maneuvers himself into an impossible situation: his actions in the service of his government are called stupid, even atrocious by the highest state authority, in the person of Baron von Schmettau, who demands an immediate solution that must, he emphasizes, in no way involve his Highness, the Prince. When the culprit, Ninon de Hauteville, who is fully aware of her power over Ströbel, refuses to cooperate, she makes him look like a fool in front of his subordinate. After Ströbel has finally realized the precarious situation he has put himself into, Hauteville demands a huge sum of money for agreeing to her own release and for quietly leaving town. Ströbel now has to do the unthinkable: he goes to Beermann, whom he had treated with contempt in his office the same day, and assisted by von Schmettau, he literally begs Beermann for help. Beermann and von Schmettau immediately develop an understanding. Both follow the same philosophy, which von Schmettau expresses with striking bluntness: "By the way, as a mere theory, all that [morals] is fine. I only do not like to see it when one does not differentiate."[17] This statement accurately sums up the message of Thoma's *Moral*: for certain people, rules of a moral and ethical nature are good only as long as they themselves do not have to live by them, at least not all the time; but for the general public, they are to be absolutely binding.

Although moral societies, at least in their old form, have long since died out, *Moral* is as pertinent today as it was in the days of Henrik Ibsen   regardless of the prevailing political or social systems.

IV   Erster Klasse *(First Class) Peasant Farce in One Act*

Josef Filser, the notorious deputy of the Bavarian Parliament, is on his way to Munich. He enters a compartment in the first-class section of a Bavarian passenger train that is already occupied by a loquacious salesman by the name of Stüve from Neuruppin; a newly married couple from North Germany, Assessor von Kleewitz and his bride, Lotte; and a high official in the Royal Bavarian government, named von Scheibler. Obviously unaware of his important position as a deputy, the passengers are annoyed by the arrival in their compartment of this seemingly rustic old farmer. Stüve informs him that he has entered a first-class compartment, suggesting that he move along into the second-class section. Filser is unperturbed. At the next station, he even invites another farmer who has boarded the train, an old friend by the name of Sylvester Gsottmaier, to join him in the first-class compartment. When the two farmers' lively conversation develops into jokes about the stupidity of government officials, von Scheibler's patience runs out. He is determined to have the two rascals thrown out of the compartment. At the next stop, von Scheibler calls for the conductor and insists that the two insolent country bumpkins be removed. To his amazement, he is quietly told by the railroad official that one of the farmers is none other than Josef Filser, the well-known deputy of Parliament. The effect this answer has on von Scheibler is almost catastrophic. Deadly embarrassed, he humbly apologizes to the two farmers for his rude behavior. After all, how could he have known to what high personage he had been talking. Filser, thoroughly enjoying von Scheibler's humiliation, assures him, in a fatherly way, that he and his friend had also not intended to insult his honor as a government official. Von Scheibler is relieved that Filser holds nothing against him, and even takes a pinch of snuff which Gsottmaier offers. But Filser is not yet finished having fun with von Scheibler, who tries, in a subservient manner, to ask him about the issues at stake in the new parliamentary session. The deputy returns von Scheibler's questions by teasing him about salaries of government officials, saying that he would personally vote against any raises, and further claims to have heard a rumor about impending personnel cuts in the government departments. He then tells Gsottmaier that people like von Scheibler often would like to bite the deputies of Parliament when the Chamber does something contrary to their liking, although their anger does little good since they are helpless against the power of Parliament.

At the station in Munich, where Filser has to get off, von Scheibler carries the deputy's basket of eggs as he helps him deboard the train, repeating his apology for the "error" all the while. After a final humble apology, the curtain falls.

Thoma began writing his *Erster Klasse* during an unhappy period of his life. His marriage was not going well, and he was distressed by the death of his good friends, Ferdinand von Reznicek and, particularly, Albert Langen. More and more he found himself in solitude, writing and hunting at the "Tuften." He felt that work alone might revive his disheartened spirits, and among the several ideas forming in his head, it was *Erster Klasse* that he first gave himself to, simply because he hoped its comic theme might help to brighten his gloomy mood.

In late spring of 1910, things began to look somewhat more encouraging, although Thoma's marital problems had not yet been

resolved. In July, shortly before the start of the hunting season, he
wrote to Ganghofer: "I am just about finished with my one-act play
about Josef Filser riding in the first-class compartment on a train to
the city. It has given me an opportunity to make great fun of the
Bavarian railroads, the pedantry of Bavarian officialdom, a traveling
salesman from Berlin, and two coarse fellows from Dachau. [This is]
a task. . . which one undertakes for one's own enjoyment; effortless
and carefree."[18] And one month later, he wrote to Ganghofer about
the imminent first performance of the play: "On Friday, August 12
[1910], the first performance of my peasant farce, *Erster Klasse*, will
take place. . . . The farce has turned out, I believe, to be robust
and funny. And a little naughtiness against the Bavarian railroad
system and the subservience of the Ministry vis-à-vis the Center
party has turned out to be uninhibited and jolly . . . the lameness
after Langen's death, the discontent with the current circumstances
in the *Simplicissimus* are overcome, and I once more become the
old 'animal,' [although] with a little [added] self-possession."[19]

When Thoma wrote *Erster Klasse*, he had one particular stage in
mind, namely the *Gasthaus zur Überfahrt* in Egern on the
Tegernsee, located only fifteen minutes from his home, where the
theater group of his friend, Michael Dengg, played almost every
evening. Dengg and his people had been dedicated to the
Volksstück for quite some time, and they were specialists in playing
the roles of country people, never making the mistake of bowing to
the demands of the public, as most theater groups do who concentrate on *Volksstücke*. They stayed away from slapstick techniques
too. Thoma first saw one of Dengg's productions during the
summer of 1908, and was strongly impressed by it. A friendship
developed between the two men which lasted until Thoma's death.
A farce like *Erster Klasse* seemed to be custom-made for the Dengg
ensemble. During the rehearsals for the first performance, Thoma
directed the play personally.[20] Michael Dengg himself played the
part of Filser, a role which suited him perfectly. On March 4, 1911,
Dengg and his troop performed *Erster Klasse* at the *Deutsches
Theater* in Munich. As expected, the play turned out to be a great
success. Famous *Volksschauspieler* (popular actors), among them
Bertl Schultes, have played the part of Filser more than a thousand
times.

Erster Klasse is as popular today as it was in Thoma's lifetime,
and especially in Bavaria. After all, none of the author's plays has so
much Bavarian flavor as this little farce, which is literally built

around an original Arch-Bavarian, the rustic deputy Josef Filser, certainly the strongest character Thoma ever created. Filser appears not only in *Erster Klasse*, but also in the so-called *Filserbriefe*. He is the personification of all the qualities Thoma either cherished or despised in the Bavarian peasant. He is straightforward, sometimes to the point of brutality, on the one hand, and crafty, on the other. He knows how to look out for himself and wants to live in peace with other people. But he never forgets anything which has been done to him by others, and he ultimately does not forgive. Generally speaking, Thoma undoubtedly had a great admiration for the character of the Bavarian peasant. He believed that the farmer retained the same moral code to which he had adhered since ancient times. At the same time, Thoma never refrained from criticizing the stubbornness of the country people, particularly during his Dachau times when he had to deal with them as a lawyer.

Filser, the individual, finds himself in a particularly interesting position. First, he is a farmer, a member of a social class which is looked down upon by anyone from the city, regardless of the latter's own social status. Secondly, he happens to hold the honorable office of an elected deputy, which he has acquired by the grace of his mentor, the parish priest of his home town, who had hand-picked him to be a candidate of the Center party. Filser's ambivalent position within the social hierarchy, coupled with his witty and cunning nature, give him many advantages over his surroundings. At home, he is a respected member of the rural community, sometimes even feared by his own neighbors. Away from home, he can travel under the fool's flag. He can stay an anonymous farmer, or he can pull rank on people as the situation requires. *Erster Klasse* is constructed around Filser's double existence: he appears in a first-class compartment looking like a clumsy fool. He is publicly humiliated by his wife, who threatens him from the platform that he will suffer consequences if he dares to return again with an empty purse. Filser's initial impact on the passengers is intensified when his friend Gsottmaier joins him in the compartment. The behavior of the two farmers seems so repulsively unrefined to the other, more cultivated passengers that it finally produces the great scene in which von Scheibler demands the removal of the two "intruders."

Filser's counterpart on the other end of the social ladder is von Scheibler, a high official in the Ministry, who never forgets his rank and status. Initially, he refuses to talk to anyone, but finally he becomes involved, first in an effort merely to ward off the attempted familiarities by Stüve and later by Filser, responding curtly to their questions as he ostensibly hides behind his unfolded newspaper; and, secondly, after having so painfully learned Filser's true identity, he behaves in exactly the opposite manner, by patronizing Filser with polite questions and by telling Stüve how much he values the farmer as an important link in society, and by repeatedly asking Filser not to hold against him the mistake of not having recognized him as the famous deputy. At the end, Filser plays the tune and von Scheibler dances—an infinitely comical situation.

As long as he lived, Thoma never tired of denouncing timeserving and opportunism. These "qualities" he had found in all too many bureaucrats during his career as a government lawyer. Already during his apprenticeship in Traunstein Thoma had met characters, like von Scheibler, who left a lasting impression on him. His first boss offered a good example. In all likelihood, he became the archetype for the bureaucrats in Thoma's plays, prose and satirical poems. In Thoma's autobiographical notes, one finds a classic description of his boss in Traunstein: "Without passion, and rude against little people, mistrusting of everybody, complacent, ignorant and garrulous, that is the kind of man who was supposed to guide me during my first steps into a world which I looked at with great respect."[21] It was this kind of *Beamter* (official) who created a deep aversion to the whole profession, especially among the country people. It is not surprising that Filser takes pleasure in teaching von Scheibler a lesson when he says to the government official: "Just be honest, you really cannot stand us." To which von Scheibler humbly replies: "Well, ah. . . if that is your conviction. . . ." And Filser says: "No, no!. . . They [the bureaucrats] sometimes do look at us out of their glasses in a way that one really knows they would like to bite us. . . ." At this point Filser and Gsottmaier laugh until the embarrassed von Scheibler joins in. Gsottmaier quips: "If they only were able to!" Filser adds: "And if they were not on a leash!"[22]

The other characters in the play have supportive functions. Von Kleewitz, a cotton-dry Prussian official, belongs to the same social class as von Scheibler. As a North German, he is full of contempt for a Bavarian farmer. He and his young bride are, however, absorbed in one another and nearly oblivious to everything around them. Their conversation throughout the play is limited to a few words. Stüve, on the other hand, contributes a bit more to the conversation. Although his ability to converse with a Bavarian farmer is somewhat limited by his Berlin background, he tries very hard to make himself understood. In spite of being a member of a lower social class than von Kleewitz, he shares the Prussian nobleman's contempt for the local populace. However, his tactless, inquisitive nature, combined with the hope of making a business deal, forces him to talk to the farmers.

Erster Klasse is probably Thoma's best comedy. He felt very comfortable in the world of Bavarian farmers who know how to deal with cityfolks. This basic theme had fascinated him already in *Die Medaille*, and it stayed with him in variations, of course, through most of his later works. Thoma's sympathies were clearly on the side of the farmer, whom he saw as the realist who lives his life without hypocrisy.

Erster Klasse has not become obsolete, but continues to be fresh and topical, first because of the appealing originality and genuineness of its characters and the realism and candor of the dialogue, and secondly because the two major contrasting elements upon which the play is based—the tensions between farmers and cityfolks and between Bavarians and North Germans—represent worlds which remain as remote and mutually misunderstood today as they were when the play was written.

With *Erster Klasse*, Thoma had reached a peak in his humoristic expression of human frailties that in all probability he recognized would be hard to reach again. It is not surprising that his next significant stage play was a tragedy.

V Magdalena *Volksstück in Three Acts*

Magdalena is the only daughter of a respectable old farmer, Thomas Mayr, who is also called Paulimann by his neighbors. Thomas has the unpleasant task of telling his dying wife, Mariann, that they must face the disgrace of having their daughter, whom they call "Leni," escorted home by the police from the city, where she has become a prostitute. Sensing her husband's sorrow and shame, and fearing that he will reject Leni out of anger, Mariann makes him promise not to abandon the girl.

At home, Leni shows little interest in keeping house for her father after her mother's death, but is usually to be found admiring herself in the mirror and daydreaming about getting married. Thomas's servant, Lenz, decides to find work elsewhere, because no one would want to live under the same roof with Leni. Mayor Lechner, a cunning old farmer, advises Thomas to sell his farm and move on, since Leni's presence is a disgrace to the town. With this insult, Thomas can no longer contain his anger. He grabs the mayor and gives him a good thrashing.

Later Thomas hears from his neighbor Plank that the townspeople are in a rage because Leni spent the night with one of the town fellows and then asked him for money. He warns Thomas to restrain his daughter, or suffer the consequences. But Thomas cannot send Leni away because he promised his dying wife not to forsake her. The town council decides to take action against Leni after hearing testimony on the matter. They demand that Thomas throw her out of his house. But Thomas will not be moved. As he sees it, it is the mayor who is responsible for the whole scandal since it was he who had Leni brought back from the city and who spread the gossip about her shameful ways. Leni is brought into the room after having tried to run away. In front of the mayor and council, Thomas demands to know if she had asked for the money. At first she denies it, and then explains that she needed money to get away from the town, where everyone thinks that she is evil. Overcome by the revelation, Thomas screams violently: "And you have done this to me!" He draws his knife and runs the blade into Magdalena's chest. Facing the people who have stepped back in horror, Thomas says in a grave voice: "Now drag her out into shame."

Thoma first considered the idea of writing a *Volksstück* during 1908, the year he developed a close friendship with Ludwig Ganghofer. Very possibly, the influence of Ganghofer's personality and art helped to put him on this track, and certainly the tragedies of Ludwig Anzengruber were a contributing element. All during 1908, Thoma familiarized himself with Anzengruber's plays, reading or watching them on the stage. The great Austrian playwright was a strong critic of the Church's role within rural society, and Thoma was deeply impressed by Anzengruber's cold realism and by the powerful figures in his plays. The peasant tragedies of Karl Schönherr, the other famous contemporary Austrian dramatist, intensified Thoma's urge to write a *Volksstück* of his own. However, it took considerable time before he could realize his plan. Marital problems which led to the dissolution of his marriage occupied his mind, and he was engaged in writing his novel *Der Wittiber*. In November 1911 he wrote to Conrad Haussmann: "How many works have I not planned, started, laid out, torn up and put aside! Plays and comedies, and now I am occupied by a

Volksstück which is going to be powerful, because it has to become powerful. It will be called *Magdalena*, and it deals with the fate of a poor peasant wench who had . . . [become] a prostitute . . . and who is brought home by the police."[23] And later he wrote: "I have put the comedy and other projected plays back into a folder, and I have started a melancholic *Volksstück*, which I will not leave unfinished and which shall prove that I can crack the mold which Berlin and Barnowsky have cast for me."[24] He wrote *Magdalena* almost out of protest against attempts to rubber-stamp him as a writer of peasant comedies. In a letter to his old friend Michael Dengg he underlined the fact that he was writing a tragedy: ". . . I am working on an Upper Bavarian [Dachauer] *Volksstück*.—No piece of fun or comical play, but a serious one; but if it goes on as it has up to now, [it will be] a juicy play.—I have delayed all comedies for Berlin. . . . Naturally, I will give you the rights for performances in Tegernsee and for some other cities you want to tour. But before August 1912 I will not let the cat out of the bag. I will revise the play several times and then let it rest again."[25] In the spring of 1912, Thoma sent the completed play to Dengg with the comment: "Dear master and miserable scoundrel! Hereby I send you *Magdalena*, so you know what you will have as baggage for your tour in fall."[26] Two months earlier, Thoma had written to Dengg with pride about the newly finished play: "Perhaps all of you have read the note in the N.N. [*Münchner Neueste Nachrichten*] about my new play. It is serious, tragic, and has power galore. Of course, you will get the play for your tour. To be sure, you will need a young person who can play a peasant wench well. . . . Try and look for something like that during the summer, then we will have a few rehearsals here together before you go on tour. You will get the main part. But that means that you will have to study like mad, and almost more than with [Anzengruber's] *Glaube und Heimat*. . . ."[27] Thoma placed greatest emphasis on the third act, where the climax and solution of a tragedy belong. He explains to his friend why he let Magdalena commit the foolish act after her return home, which in turn brings final judgment upon her as the only possible way out of the mud which she had irretrievably sunken into: "Here I send you the third act. I think that it comes out even stronger than the second one. . . . Out of the father's deep anxiety, his anger and desperation, results the ending, which has to produce a redeeming and liberating effect. The death of the father would not accomplish that, because what happens then? The listener would have the painful and unsatisfactory feeling that the stupid woman was now to face the beginning of an endless series of misery, shame and stupidity. This way it is a *causa finita*."[28] Not only the third act has this genuinely tragic quality to offer; the first and the second also show the author as a master of the truly classic tragedy. Long before the premiere, Thoma remarked: "I do, myself, certainly know that I have created something good with *Magdalena*, and that I have extended the limits which critics and experts of literature have set for me."[29]

Magdalena was well received on the stage. It was first performed in the *Kleines Theater* in Berlin, again with Viktor Barnowsky as the director, on October 12, 1912. Seven days later it came out at Munich's *Residenztheater* under the direction of Friedrich Basil. Soon the Munich public knew *Magdalena* as the Bavarian *Emilia Galotti*. It was certainly a great compliment for Thoma to be compared with the venerable Lessing. However, particularly in Berlin, where Thoma had already been celebrated on several occasions as a favorite of the theatergoing public, the interest in *Magdalena* began to taper off after a while, and faster than expected. Thoma commented bitterly to Michael Dengg, with whom he now shared the familiar "Du" address; "I also want to thank you for the news about the peasant wench, *Magdalena*, who seems to be not as stimulating for the North Germans as is the Viennese operetta junk. But, I am still glad that I am the father."[30] Thoma was convinced that he had written a good play, and he was in no need of any public certification of his abilities as a dramatist. Although the plot of *Magdalena* deals with a human tragedy which is caused by a prevailing moral code as it existed around the turn of the century, its characters are by no means subject to changing modes and fashions. Magdalena herself is an immutable figure. As the forces of nemesis descend on her, she seems irrevocably condemned, given up by society, and she emerges as nothing more than a stupid, deplorable slut. Everything she does after her return from the city produces annoyance, as she sinks deeper into guilt every day. She does not arouse the viewer's compassion immediately, because she appears continuously reluctant to start a new life for herself by following her parents' advice. Her corrupted soul is not receptive to her father's rough, but benevolent, attempts to keep her out of trouble. But what is it really that got her into such a state of mind in which redemption is virtually impossible? The father's answer is clear and unmistakable: both disillusionment and naive stupidity. The father, on the other hand, has the full sympathy and support of the viewer. He is the one who takes up the struggle with the overwhelming powers of fate, and he is the one who will ultimately be crushed by them. He is not overly protective of his daughter; on the contrary, he wishes that she had never come home. He is even tempted to send her back to the city. The only real reason for his determination in fighting the mayor and the townspeople who want to do away with Magdalena, is the promise he made to his dying wife not to forsake Leni, however great the adversities. By virtue of that promise, which he intends to keep, he puts himself into the position of a man who defend his child, not for its own sake, but for the purpose of fulfilling a sacred pledge. He does not really believe that Magdalena, as a human being, is worthy of his protection. But at the deathbed of his wife, he is made to realize that regardless of her moral turpitude, Leni is his daughter, and that he would have to stand up for her against the whole world if it were to demand her expulsion. When he must chose between his daughter's total mental destruction and her death, he kills her, thereby letting her at least die without further shame. The ending of *Magdalena* is worthy of an ancient tragedy and lives up to the high standards which Lessing set for the German *Trauerspiel*: fear, horror and compassion are aroused in the viewer to a high degree. No other figure in *Magdalena* demands as much compassion as Thomas does. He not only has to fight the whole town and its self-righteousness, but he also has to defend himself against the intrigues of a personal enemy, the town mayor, who is taking revenge for a court battle which he lost to Thomas many years before. A stiff moral code, enthusiastically enforced by a hateful enemy, causes the ruin of both Thomas and Magdalena. 2/9/35

Magdalena is a true *Volksstück*, but it is without exaggerated sentimentality, something one usually associates with plays of this genre. Thomas, the main character, is a genuine Bavarian farmer, a man who stands with both feet firmly on the ground; a realist who is capable of facing the truth. At the same time, this strong-willed man has compassion, which does not allow him to let his child be trampled upon, unworthy as she might be. Thomas bears his tragic fate in a truly manly way until the load becomes impossible to carry. His action ends his own suffering, as well as his daughter's.

CHAPTER 3

Novels and Novellas

I Andreas Vöst

A NDREAS Vöst is a respected farmer in Erlbach, a small town in Upper Bavaria. He is well liked by almost everybody except the parish priest, Reverend Baustätter, who cannot forget that it was Vöst who prevented him from building a new church spire, by persuading the townspeople to turn against the project. From that time on, the priest has seen in Andreas Vöst a bitter enemy on whom he would relish taking revenge. The opportunity presents itself before long, after Vöst's newborn child, a baby girl, dies shortly after her birth. When Vöst asks the priest to baptize the infant posthumously, he refuses. Vöst has to bury the child outside the walls of the churchyard, while Baustätter celebrates his first triumph over his enemy. But Vöst remains an unbroken man. Bad luck soon strikes again, however, when it is discovered that his young daughter, Ursula, has become pregnant without the benefit of marriage. The father of the child, according to Ursula, is Xaver Hierangl, the son of a man who also wishes Andreas Vöst no good. But young Hierangl denies the relationship with Vöst's daughter, even after Vöst roughs him up. Reverend Baustätter, not wishing to miss another opportunity to deride Vöst, makes subtle references to Vöst's domestic troubles in his sermon on the following Sunday. To add insult to injury, Vöst learns, after his mother's sudden death, that she designated a large sum of money for the new church spire in her will.

Things suddenly seem to look better for Andreas Vöst when he is elected mayor of Erlbach, with the help of the *Bauernbund* (farmer's union), a new and rapidly growing political movement. As mayor, it would be easy for him to effectively fight the parish priest. But Baustätter, who is horrified by the thought of Vöst's newly acquired power, spreads a rumor among the townspeople that Vöst is such a cruel and heartless man that he used to beat his old father, who is since deceased. As proof, he submits a memorandum supposedly written by his predecessor, the late Reverend Held, who was a man widely known and deeply respected by the people. Baustätter sends the memorandum, which is actually a forgery, to the district supervisor, asking him not to confirm Vöst as the new mayor because of his evil nature. The supervisor, a spineless opportunist, welcomes any chance to weaken the movement of the *Bauernbund* by not permitting one of its members to become a town mayor. He gladly complies with the priest's request and refuses confirmation of Vöst as the new mayor of Erlbach. Vöst's old enemy, Hierangl, is appointed instead. All of the protests and complaints which Vöst registers are in vain. Like Josef K. in Kafka's *Trial*, he has to realize that no one will listen to him and his cause. Following the advice of his friends, he finally gives up. But soon the old feud between Vöst and the priest resumes when Vöst's wife brings her daughter's illegitimate child to Baustätter to be baptized. The priest insists on the name "Simplizius" for the baby. A name like "Simpl" would be a humiliation for the child all its life.

With the help of Sylvester Mang, a former student of theology who has seen the falsified memo concerning Vöst's alleged moral turpitude, Vöst asks for a reinvestigation of his case which denied him the mayorship. But the supervisor flatly refuses to reconsider, saying that it is not the ominous memo, but the widespread acceptance of its content that has made his confirmation impossible. Mang urges Vöst to pursue the matter in court, but Vöst gives up again. Like Kleist's Michael Kohlhaas, he knows that there is no way for him to fight the evil web of lies and rumors spun around him. Physical force would be the only way to contend, but he is too tired to be violent. In his mind, he closes his own case and goes home. On Easter Sunday, the most sacred feast in Catholic Bavaria, Andreas Vöst is seen in the tavern already in the morning, drinking and brooding. He does not even go home to eat the blessed Easter meal, but is still sitting in the tavern as the afternoon guests arrive, among whom he sees his archenemy, Hierangl. Worried about his unusual drinking bout, Andreas's wife sends her son, Seppl, to the tavern to bring her husband home. When Seppl arrives, he finds his father entangled in an argument with Hierangl. He tries to restrain his father, and resorts to force to prevent a fight. For a moment it appears as if father and son were engaged in a brawl. Seeing this, Hierangl reminds Andreas Vöst, triumphantly and at the top of his voice, that Seppl is now doing the same thing to Vöst that Vöst had once done to his own father, just as the disputed memorandum had charged. Losing control of himself, Vöst grabs a beer mug and throws it at Hierangl's forehead with great force. Hierangl falls to the floor, unconscious. On the next morning, he dies, and Vöst is placed under arrest.

At the trial, which is held in Nussbach, the district town, Andreas Vöst has to go through a new series of disappointments and frustrations because the judges seem only to want to listen to the softspoken Reverend Baustätter, who claims that he had consistently offered understanding and compassion to all of the members of his parish, including Andreas Vöst. He testifies that despite his efforts, he soon had to witness the moral decay in Vöst's home, and that the exceedingly violent Vöst has now murdered the father of four children. When Vöst is finally asked whether he has any comment to make, he is only able to point at Reverend Baustätter and say: "He is responsible for everything." The final irony for Andreas Vöst comes when, as he begins to serve his four-year prison term, workers erect a scaffolding around Erlbach's old church spire. The new spire will be built after all.

Andreas Vöst is Thoma's first novel, and it is a powerful one. It appeared during 1905, a year which marked a high point in Thoma's life in several ways. He had already established himself as a playwright; he had just returned from his extensive journey through southern France, northern Africa, and Sicily; and he was in love with Marietta, whom he would marry the same year. A new and exciting life lay before him. With full enthusiasm, he threw himself into the milieu which he both knew and enjoyed so thoroughly: the world of the farmers around his former home, Dachau. This time his beloved peasants were to be dealt with in a formidable prose work, an undertaking he had longed to embark on for many years. In contrast to the plays which he had been producing since 1899, he wanted this novel to become a serious piece, free of humor, laughter and satire. It should show the hard, even brutal and merciless, side of one farmer's life and struggle against his enemies, and his eventual demise, brought about by a cold and revengeful priest.

The figures in *Andreas Vöst* are all drawn in a lifelike manner, and the piercing realism with which they are portrayed overwhelms the reader. Andreas Vöst towers above all the other figures in the novel. He is a straightforward and industrious man who has worked hard all his life to earn what he possesses. Had it not been for his opposition to the priest's project to build a new church spire, he probably would have ended up an honorable patriarch, well liked and respected by everyone. Vöst had certainly never been a religious devotee, but he had had a good relationship with Reverend Held, Baustätter's predecessor, whom he saw as the ideal of the good priest, a dedicated shepherd who understands the needs of his flock.

Kind and humane clergymen like Reverend Held were truly the backbone of the Catholic Church, especially in rural areas. They enjoyed the trust and cooperation of their parishioners and were fully credible as spiritual leaders. But there was also another type of clergyman present in Bavaria when Thoma wrote his *Andreas Vöst:* the power-hungry, intolerant, and revengeful priest. And this led to the dominant theme in Thoma's first novel: anticlericalism and politics.

The reader of *Andreas Vöst* gets the impression throughout this work that Thoma had an axe to grind with the clergy and its social and political ambitions. When Thoma worked on the novel, his involvement in the battles of the *Simplicissimus* with its self-chosen enemies was reaching its peak. He had allowed himself to become entangled in a multitude of public issues, ranging from the snobbishness of Wilhelm II and its effect on German politics, to the daily life of the German petit bourgeois. Considering the increasing enthusiasm which he displayed in his frequent attacks against the establishment, it was only natural for him to develop a tendency to overkill. He generated a certain intolerance combined with an almost galloping heavy-handedness, such as is characteristic of a fanatic; for that is precisely what Thoma had become since he had started to contribute to the *Simplicissimus* in 1899. During these years at the *Simplicissimus,* Thoma, who had always possessed a healthy sense for detecting phoniness, increasingly adopted a stance in opposition to the political establishment, the national institutions, and especially to the government and the Church. It was particularly the "unholy" alliance of Church and State which he began to denounce in short satiric poems and in the *Filserbriefe.* Thoma had written himself into a rage, and he waged a crusade against the "evil" state and against "this nation of opportunists," which, according to him, could be changed for the better only by responsible socialism. But he saw no possibility for this change as long as the churches and their power-hungry clergy, regardless of their denomination, were perpetuating the status quo.

In this spirit, Reverend Baustätter was conceived as the epitome of the evil priest who, in cooperation with the political powers, rules over his flock both physically and spiritually. Baustätter has his confidants everywhere in and around the village. They literally allow him to see into the souls of his parishioners. Whenever somebody stands up against him, he uses his clerical powers against him. He manipulates intimidated people and does not even hesitate to forge a document in order to incriminate his enemy. The Reverend is not only an evil man, he is also a hypocrite. The books in his library are displayed merely to impress his guests. One thick volume, the history of the saints, is placed conspicuously in the immediate view of every visitor, suggesting heavy use by its appearance. During prayer, he and his chaplain give a saintly impression, but they treat ordinary people either in a humiliating and patronizing way, or they shout at them in anger. Baustätter himself frequently flies into a "sacred rage," like Moses in the Old Testament. It becomes quite obvious that he is a despicable character, a wolf in sheep's clothing. His diabolic personality not only influences the fate of his immediate enemies, but in the case of Andreas Vöst it also has an indirect effect on people who are initially not involved in his intrigues. A good example is Sylvester Mang, the former student of theology. To a large degree, it is the negative example of Baustätter which brings about Mang's decision not to become a priest, since he does not want to have such colleagues.

If one superficially summarizes what has been said about this novel, one might see it as the story of a farmer who dares to stand up against a representative of the Church. In return, this representative of the Church brings about the farmer's downfall. The evil manner in which the priest appears in the novel, however, makes *Andreas Vöst* seem rather to be an anticlerical work, full of ideological and political polemics. Undoubtedly, Thoma was not fully aware of the harmful effects this could have on the literary stature of the novel, particularly since he did not intend his first narrative to be a political pamphlet. All he really wanted to do was to present an objective picture of Southern Bavaria's rural life in the nineties of the past century. In a letter to Conrad Haussmann, he expressed this in rather definite terms: "My novel is proceeding nicely; a fast pace is naturally impossible when one works carefully. The development of the story itself would not be as difficult as that of the characters. . . . No untruth and no phrase is allowed to sneak in. . . . I have now completed about eight chapters; there will be about sixteen. Besides the personal experiences of the individual, there will be political history, the *Bauernbund*, the position of the district supervisor, etc. The whole thing should also give a true picture of the times. I am working with enthusiasm and joy."[1]

As far as the language of *Andreas Vöst* is concerned, Thoma certainly reached the goal he had set for himself: there are no phrases or clichés in the entire novel. Even the dialogues set in Bavarian dialect are entirely genuine. They depict conversations between country people the way one can still hear them today: short and straight to the point, free of superfluous niceties or generalities. Everything has its place in the mind and also in the mouth of every farmer or farm woman. There are scenes containing little jewels of narration, such as the casual talk between the midwife and the waitress in the tavern, or the one in which Andreas Vöst asks the priest to bury his infant child in the churchyard because his wife desires it. One has the distinct feeling that these people do not say one useless word, and one even imagines their faces or their gestures as one reads the dialogue. Thoma's superb ability to depict a real situation proved itself in a distinctly masterful way in this, his first larger work in prose, as it had before in his plays.

Had Thoma not been carried away by his zeal to teach both the clergy and the Bavarian bureaucracy a lesson, *Andreas Vöst* would probably have become a novel worthy of Jeremias Gotthelf. In one's overall judgment, one should certainly not go as far as Soergel / Hohoff, who argue that *Andreas Vöst*, which could have become a monumental *Volksroman*, ends as a "hardly believable detective story."[2] This judgment is too harsh and cannot be supported by facts if one looks at a common definition of a detective story. First of all, nothing that happens in *Andreas Vöst* is in any way mysterious. The story unfolds in escalating actions and reactions, and the homicide at the end is a very probable consequential action in the eyes of anyone who is familiar with life in the Bavarian countryside. It remains a fact, however, that the novel shows one deficiency which prevents it from becoming a literary masterwork, namely its tendency to be all-too-obvious. The final classification of *Andreas Vöst* lies somewhere between a classic *Bauernroman*, an ideological and political satire, and a detective story. It is a piece of prose written with a thorough knowledge of the Bavarian people, executed in an ingeniously transparent style, but infected by the raging fire of ideologically motivated anger.

II   Der Wittiber *(The Widower)*

An Upper Bavarian farmer named Schormayer is deeply sadden-
ed by the death of his wife. Bewildered, he seems not to know what
to do with himself; his life has lost its meaning and direction. When
he can no longer endure the meaningless questions and condolences
offered by the guests at the dinner being held at the *Gasthaus*
following the funeral, in the manner traditional in the Bavarian
countryside, he decides to go home. When he arrives at his house
and his female servant, Zenzi, tries to comfort him, he realizes for
the first time what a handsome and well-built woman she is. When
she sits down next to him, he cannot refrain from grabbing her. But
she quickly escapes his embrace when she hears noises from outside.
Schormayer's daughter, Ursula, enters the room, and recognizing
that she has surprised the two, she angrily tells Zenzi to leave.
Schormayer tells his daughter in no uncertain terms to mind her
own business; he is, after all, master of the house. She quietly
retreats, but in the days that follow she secretly has her father
watched by a neighbor whom she hires on the pretext of needing an
additional female servant in the house. Everything seems to return
to normal until one evening when Schormayer returns from visiting
a friend in another village. In good spirits for the first time since his
wife's funeral, he enters the darkened house and in the candlelight
sees Zenzi standing at the top of the staircase, only half dressed.
Again he cannot restrain himself, and inevitable happens. Ursula
comes home shortly afterwards and discovers that her father is in
the maid's room. Schormayer ignores Zenzi's warning to be quiet as
he leaves her room, and makes plenty of noise as he slams the door
behind him and stomps down the stairs, as if to demonstrate that he
does as he pleases as the master in the house. But he has already
firmly decided that Zenzi must go, because an affair with a servant
is unthinkable in a farmer's household.

On the next morning during breakfast, another scene occurs
between Ursula and Zenzi during which Ursula threatens to throw
the immoral servant out of the house. But Schormayer, not in the
least humbled or embarrassed by the events of the previous night,
shouts at his daughter, telling her, once and for all, that he will have
Zenzi stay. Shortly afterwards, another heated debate takes place
between Schormayer and his son, Lenz, whom his sister has in the
meantime informed about all the happenings. But the father clearly
emerges as the victor after telling Lenz to pack his things and leave

should he dare to talk so disrespectfully again, and adding that Lenz's insolence has made him decide that Zenzi will definitely stay in the house.

From that moment on, no peace is possible in the Schormayer house. The air has been poisoned by hatred. Although Schormayer's mind is occupied by the logging which has to be done during the winter months, he well knows that something has to happen in regard to Zenzi, in order to restore tranquillity and order in the house. The situation begins to improve when Ursula starts making plans to leave to get married. Before long, however, Zenzi confesses that she is pregnant. Since Schormayer cannot talk to her about the sensitive matter at home, he meets her in the woods to work out a settlement. He tells her that she must leave the house and marry a young lad. But Zenzi maintains that she has no boyfriend, and that she wants the child to have a name when it comes into the world. Schormayer realizes that further discussion is futile and permits her to stay in the house, at least for the time being. But this does not prove to be a good solution at all. Lenz, whose anger and suspicion are growing daily, gets into a fight with Hansgirgl, the old and trusted servant of the house, whom he accuses of being his father's spy. The servant, deeply insulted, leaves the farm for good, much to Schormayer's annoyance. Again Schormayer makes an unsuccessful attempt to get Zenzi to leave since she is already showing signs of her pregnancy. During Ursula's wedding banquet, Schormayer and Lenz have another fight after the father calls his son a fool in front of the guests. In spite of this humiliation, the young man makes one more attempt to talk to his father the next day. But the prevailing mood does not permit any rational discussion between the two. They begin shouting at each other, and Schormayer tells his son that he does not want him in his house any longer. Losing control of himself for a moment, Lenz grabs his father by his coat, whereupon Schormayer tells his son that he never wants to see him again.

The next day's weather promises to be beautiful as Schormayer starts out early to plow the fields. When he asks his new servant whether he has seen Lenz, he gets a negative answer. Out on the field, Schormayer realizes that things cannot go on as before, and decides to make peace with Lenz. How surprised the young fellow would be after yesterday's quarrel! It would not hurt the lad to have realized that his father could still stand on his own feet. Still occupied with such thoughts, Schormayer looks down on his farm and on the village, peacefully lying in the spring sun. But suddenly he sees pigeons flying up from the house. Thinking something must have frightened them, he returns to the house, where he finds Zenzi hanging from a roof spar of the barn and Lenz standing nearby, trembling all over.

In the fall of the same year, Schormayer sells his farm. After his son is sentenced to a long term in the penitentiary, he moves to Dachau and takes to drinking.

The critics who saw flaws in Thoma's first novel, *Andreas Vöst*, especially concerning the homogeneity of the story, may have been at least partially right. *Der Wittiber*, however, is free of any such shortcomings. Thoma had mastered German prose, and he had given the world a gem of a novel. Or is it one? If one applies a literary definition, one would rather tend to call *Der Wittiber* an epic story. Thoma himself did not want to call it a novel. He was fully aware of the fact that he had created something rather timeless and free of political tendency:

I am sitting here in the middle of the most beautiful winter and the most beautiful work. My peasant story,—novel is not the appropriate word for it—grows and prospers like a well-planted apple tree. The good qualities which you had once found in *Vöst* have probably been enhanced [in the new work]; the mistakes have been evaded. . . . [It is] a story of human events. Passions, without phrases, which develop genuinely throughout, take their effect on the plot and enhance it. And [all of it is] very old-Bavarian. Whoever will have read this book, *Der Wittiber*, will be able to say of himself that he knows quite a bit of the Old Bavarians. Also about their language. The story is growing by itself to a larger size than I could have anticipated, but I hope to finish it in four to five weeks. Sometimes I am writing a chapter in one to one-and-a-half days; sometimes I need a week to finish it. Every chapter is a picture by itself. . . .[3]

There is, indeed, not very much that even the most critical reader can add to these comments which Thoma makes about his own book. From whichever angle one looks at it, it is a true masterwork. The language is precise, piercing in its conciseness and accuracy, totally realistic in its dialect portions, absolutely free of mannerism, which always represents the greatest danger to a writer who uses dialect in his works. Thoma shows precisely how the farmers around Dachau speak, and the author's comment about getting to know the country people and their language by reading *Der Wittiber* is by no means an exaggeration. Classifying the work by its language alone, one would have to count it among the prose of literary Naturalism in Germany. But *Der Wittiber* like the works of Jeremias Gotthelf, certainly lacks the narrowness of a typical naturalistic piece.[4]Like Gotthelf, Thoma builds a wide epic arch reaching from the funeral of Schormayer's wife to the commission of the crime, which takes place as an almost inevitable consequence of an accidental misdeed. The reader never feels bored by long stretches of narrative prose because much of the story reveals itself in the dramatic dialogue of Thoma's characters, reminiscent of the figures in an Egger-Lienz painting. The plot itself reminds the reader of medieval epics. Not unlike Andreas Vöst, Schormayer almost willfully embarks on the road to his own decline, tempting the powers of fate. It is the legendary stubbornness of the free Bavarian peasant, a legacy inherited from his Teutonic ancestors, which the author wants to exhibit and demonstrate in the person of his hero. Nobody, especially not his own children, will tell the patriarch what to do, even when he is fully aware of his own wrongdoing. Although Thoma lets his hero perish—at least in an indirect, but therefore all the more painful way, as he takes to drinking—he distinctly admires the stubbornness which despises compromise and humiliation for the sake of survival. Schormayer not only does not listen to the warnings of his son and daughter which are sounded in a youthfully unwise and clumsy manner, but he also disregards the gossip of the village people which finally pushes his son into murdering Zenzi.

Lenz and Ursula, each in their own way, are foolish young people. Ursula rebels against her father only because she feels threatened by Zenzi as the new mistress of the house. Her reasons for fighting the servant are not entirely moralistic. Jealousy is the driving force for her outrage and hostility. When Ursula leaves the house to be married, she suddenly ceases to be concerned about her father's spiritual welfare which she had seen endangered by his presumed affair with the servant. At her wedding banquet, she even tries to appease her brother about the situation which has become less interesting to her now that she has left the house. Recognizing this, Lenz becomes even more enraged by Ursula's attempts to calm him down. He sees himself as the true and only loser in the family. This feeling intensifies when he listens to the gossiping old women at the dinner table. Since his father has disowned him, he has nothing more to lose and will be driven to the murder of his alleged competitor. He is certainly not an evil individual, but, like his father, a very stubborn one.

Zenzi is the more innocent victim of the crime. Surely she does not deserve death for what she has done. Her only sin was in teasing Schormayer on the evening of his wife's funeral, arousing his erotic interest in her which was later fulfilled in a more convenient and slightly drunken moment. Zenzi may have had concrete designs on the master of the house, but her plans did not include the total disruption of relations between the father and his two children. However, is it merely Zenzi's erotic bearing which lets the father forget his status and causes him to sleep with a girl who is his servant? Most certainly not, especially if one considers his strong, but cautious nature. It is Zenzi's extraordinary attractiveness among the young country girls, not to say her beauty, which forces Schormayer to take the pernicious step. Similar to Lene in Gerhart Hauptmann's novella "Bahnwärter Thiel," she has an overwhelming fascination for Schormayer, although only up to the calamitous night. Like some of Friedrich Hebbel's heroines—particularly Agnes Bernauer—she becomes guilty in the eyes of Fate by virtue of her extraordinary beauty, and her destruction becomes inevitable.

Der Wittiber is as true as life in the Bavarian countryside. Josef Hofmiller is entirely correct in his assessment of the novel when he says that *Der Wittiber* "will be more important to later generations concerning the knowledge of old-Bavarian peasanthood in our time than all of the folkloristic studies."[5] Not much can be added to that statement. With *Der Wittiber*, his best work in prose, Ludwig Thoma joined the ranks of the great epic writers.

III   Der Ruepp

Michael Umbricht, called "der Ruepp," is a weak man who tends to be boisterous. He frequently drinks too much, particularly on Sundays. Sitting half drunk in the *Gasthaus*, he starts to insult the other guests until one of them finally punches him in the nose. The proprietor tells him to leave the premises. Totally inebriated and with a bloody nose, he starts to walk home, but on his way he stumbles into a field where he falls asleep. His youngest son, Michel, finds him and brings him home. Michel, who is a nice but not-too-bright fellow, has just returned from the *Gymnasium* in Freising where, against his will, his father sent him nine years earlier to become a priest. Lacking the respect of his fellow farmers, "der Ruepp" hoped to regain their regard by having his son become a priest, and has been looking forward to the day when his son would celebrate Mass in the village church. But Michel has no aptitude for studying; he would rather work with his hands. In Freising, he feels like a prisoner. Now he has also renewed an old friendship with Stasi, the neighbor's daughter, whom he sees on his way home from the train station. Since he has already had to repeat one year in the *Gymnasium*, his headmaster let him know at the end of the semester that it would be best for him not to return in the fall. All this he tells Loni, the family's faithful servant, who lies confined in her bed, fatally ill and awaiting death. She has always been fond of the boy, whom she raised like her own child. Now she wants to help her protégé, who fears his father's reaction to his failing in school. With the money she has saved, Loni wants to enable Michel to enter the agricultural college in Weihenstephan. There he would be independent and could become a respectable manager of an estate or a large farm later on. She asks Michel to go to Dachau to bring the notary to her bedside because his presence will be needed for her to make out her will. Michel prepares to go to Dachau on his bike, but is prevented from leaving by his father, who insists that work must first be done on the farm. Afterwards, the father says, he will go for the notary himself. In the meantime, a bailiff from the court appears to collect a penalty which was imposed on "der Ruepp" in a court case which he lost to a horse trader out of negligence.

Afraid of getting deeper into debt, "der Ruepp" makes an attempt to change Loni's mind regarding her will, urging her to leave her savings to him instead of to Michel. After Loni's adamant refusal, "der Ruepp" again delays his trip to Dachau. Finally, he goes, but gets embroiled in a card game with horse traders who cheat him out of a large sum of money. He ultimately gets thrown out of the tavern and misses the notary's office hours. Half drunk, he returns home. Concerned that Michel might hear about his shameful escapade in town, he prevents his son from going for the notary for several days, claiming that there is too much harvest work to be done. When he finally gives in to the insistent pleas of his wife, Afra, to let Michel go, it is too late. Old Loni, frightened and in despair, dies during the same afternoon. Now "der Ruepp" faces a double disaster since by his fault Loni has died without a will, and neither Michel nor he will inherit her money. Loni's distant relative, a clerk named Pfleiderer, who has spent some time behind bars because of fraudulent dealings, will be the legitimate heir instead. However, "der Ruepp" does not want this to happen. Not paying any regard to Loni, who is still lying on her deathbed, he enters her room and searches her belongings, among which he finds a statement of liability in the amount of three thousand marks which he had made out to Loni several years before when he had borrowed the money from her to pay for Michel's studies in Freising. Wrapped in the same piece of paper, he also discovers several savings bonds amounting to sixteen hundred marks, and some coins. Quickly he puts everything with the exception of the coins into his pocket. When his wife enters, she finds him praying at Loni's bed. She is surprised and suspicious when she sees her husband in such a humble pose.

After Loni's burial, "der Ruepp" dutifully hands her belongings over to the village mayor. In the meantime, Michel, who has not yet told his father about his having failed in school, gets into new trouble. Accompanied by Zotzen-Peter, who is "der Ruepp's" new servant, he gets caught while trying to climb into a girl's window in a neighboring village at night. Not only does he get roughed up by the village lads, but his reputation in town is now totally ruined. A future priest simply does not get into such a predicament. At least temporarily, he is saved from his father's anger, however, when an official letter from the court orders "der Ruepp" to appear in matters concerning Loni's estate. Pfleiderer, the lawful heir to Loni's estate, not only challenges "der Ruepp's statement concerning Loni's possessions, but also wants to sue him for six thousand marks, a sum about twice the value of the money "der Ruepp" actually took from Loni's room. There is only one way out of this dilemma for "der Ruepp": he and his wife will have to testify under oath that there was no money in Loni's estate except for the cash he handed in to the mayor after the burial. For days, he tries to no avail to persuade Afra to help him out of this situation by committing perjury. She will not sacrifice her soul's salvation by committing such a deadly sin. Now "der Ruepp" makes one last attempt to save himself. He goes to his old enemy, the farmer Lukas, and offers to sell him a piece of land which Lukas had wanted to buy several years earlier. But Lukas is no longer interested in the property. Deeply depressed, "der Ruepp" proceeds to drown his misery in alcohol. His wife finds him drunk in a field and brings him home. For the first time, she recognizes that her husband is a desperate and entirely broken man. Her sympathies are aroused. She warms up some soup for him, but when she returns to his room a few minutes later, he is gone. Deeply concerned, she alarms the children and the servants, but "der Ruepp" seems to have vanished.

In the morning, a neighbor's servant finds him hanging from a tree in a nearby forest. He had put an end to his miserable existence. His son, Michel, will remain a servant all his life. The people call him "the Latin farmhand" and never quite accept him again. Stasi, the girl he loves, marries another farmer one year after "der Ruepp's" suicide.

Der Ruepp, which was written during the first four months of 1921, was to be Thoma's last work. He died three months after finishing it. Although the author was not aware of the severeness of his ailment at the time he was working on *Der Ruepp*, the novel has all the marks of a swansong. In this work Thoma carries his prose to absolute perfection. Earlier, he had observed a certain Spartan brevity of expression in his language, but in *Der Ruepp* precision and transparency reach a peak. It is difficult to find similar qualities in the prose of any modern German author. Only Theodor Fontane seems to match Thoma's stylistic precision to some extent. It is no coincidence that he was one of Ludwig Thoma's idols.

In *Der Ruepp*, as in *Der Wittiber*, Thoma combined a truly realistic prose style with a rapidly moving, quasidramatic narration. His late prose is like a fresh green mountain stream: crystal clear and swift, but without violent rapids. It should be remembered, however, that Thoma's work on *Der Ruepp* was accompanied by the same birth pangs that every author has to experience when writing a novel of this size.[6]

Unlike Andreas Vöst or Schormayer, the hero of this story is not an honorable fellow who is destroyed by the powers of fate. "Der Ruepp" is a miserable liar and a weakling from the start, a man who tries to hide his laziness and indecision with big words and aggressive behavior. The combination of weakness and brutality gets him deeper and deeper into trouble. When he sees his creditors closing in on him, he even takes to stealing and perjury, trying to cover one evil with an even bigger one. He has lost respect, not only in his family, but also in the community, and he thinks he can buy it back from Fate by having his son become a priest. But he has to learn that honor cannot be purchased. In pursuing his lost honor, he becomes callous and unfeeling toward his wife and children, as well as toward poor Loni. Although he shows no compassion for anyone, he wants to command it for himself, especially from his wife, whom he even wants to force into swearing a false oath. When she refuses, his scheme of lies falls apart. Unable to face the painful consequences—which Andreas Vöst so bravely does—"der Ruepp" takes refuge in cowardly suicide, leaving his disgraced family in a state of near-poverty. Even in death, this man finds no honor. He is never willing to accept the blame for his own failures.

The supporting figures in *Der Ruepp*—the family members, the friends, and even his enemies—are of somewhat lesser significance than they are in previous prose works. There is Afra, "der Ruepp's" wife, a devout Catholic, industrious and quiet, seemingly born to suffer the misfortunes brought upon her by her husband's misdeeds. Fate has cheated her out of a decent life with a good man, but she patiently endures whatever comes to her. Her children, particularly Kaspar, the oldest son, and Leni, her daughter, show less tolerance of their father's behavior and his negligent handling of the farm business. They both see that "der Ruepp" is running the farm into debt and openly show their disgust at more than one occasion, to no avail, of course. Michel, the student who cannot go back to school, never wanted to become a priest in the first place. He is a quiet and good-natured young fellow, but his clumsiness and naiveté get him into trouble. His hope of becoming a farm manager and his wish to take Stasi as his wife are doomed from the beginning because of his father's irresponsible bearing. Michel is in a most difficult position: he knows that he will never finish school because he has neither the will nor the mental capacity to become a theologian. He feels that his future lies in farming, but in spite of his dedication, he is never taken seriously by his parents or by the other farmers who see him as a fellow who could never hold up under the physical strains of farm work. For the rest of his life, he will be known as "the Latin farmhand."

In *Der Ruepp*, unlike in Thoma's earlier works, especially in *Andreas Vöst*, the parish priest emerges as a very positive figure. He is a pleasant, elderly gentleman, large in stature and with a sharp eye for the needs and capabilities of his parishioners. As a gourmet, he understands the desires of people for the pleasures in life, and he shows remarkable tolerance in the face of Michel's foolish mistakes, which he talks about with fatherly kindness.

Among the other figures, none attains any real significance, with the exception of the cattle agent Schlehlein, who heavily contributes to "der Ruepp's" final downfall by talking him into taking part in the disastrous cardgame during which "der Ruepp" gets cheated. Schlehlein is a distasteful fellow. Like his companions in the trade, he is full of contempt for farmers, disregarding the fact that he makes his living off them. He not only makes it his business to get to know every individual in the district and the livestock they own, but he also wants to find out all the personal circumstances of his clients, their family quarrels, their affairs, and their worries. From "der Ruepp," he extracts the purpose of his obviously important trip to Dachau right in the middle of harvest time, and later, after a fight with "der Ruepp," he uses his knowledge of Loni's estate against him by telling Pfleiderer about it, thus enabling the latter to claim his inheritance.

IV Kaspar Lorinser

For many years, Thoma had felt an overwhelming desire to write a great prose work, the *summa* of all his novels and short stories, a "quasi-autobiography," similar to Gottfried Keller's *Der grüne Heinrich*. In this definitive work in the form of an *Entwicklungsroman*, Thoma planned to reflect not only the significant turns in his own life, but also his dreams, desires, and plans, whether or not they had materialized. Most importantly, it was to capture, in almost cosmic breath, life as it existed in his beloved "Old Bavaria" of the eighteen-seventies and eighties, which he so painfully missed since his early adult years. The whole novel was to be fed by the never-fading impressions of his childhood, when the irretrievable aura of happy times still prevailed. Briefly, it was a concept whose motor was to be nostalgia, undoubtedly the most beautiful driving force behind any work of art. But were dreams enough for a realist like Thoma to write the poetic summary of his life? In the spring of 1921, after one year of working on the novel, Thoma expressed his disappointment with the subject in a few undramatic words in a letter to Josef Hofmiller: "In the meantime, *Lorinser* is lying in the drawer and is waiting for its resurrection [which will take place] perhaps in the fall. It suffers from a major organic flaw. One cannot 'invent' an autobiography; something like that becomes false and agonizing. One can only write things one has lived through, things one has thought oneself. . . ."[7]

Kaspar Lorinser's story begins somewhat like Thoma's own: he grows up in the mountainous countryside of Upper Bavaria; but unlike Thoma he is the son of a farmer. Other "inventions" follow: in his early school years, the teacher recognizes Kaspar as a gifted youngster, and his mother and grandmother are persuaded to send him to the *Gymnasium* in Burghausen, a small town on the Austrian border. There the two women find a place for him to stay with distant relatives. Although terribly unhappy and homesick for his beloved mountains, Kaspar slowly gets used to the new life-style. At this point, the story abruptly ends.

Thoma had hinted to Hofmiller that he might resume work on the novel later, but he never actually did. The torso contains exceedingly beautiful passages, particularly when the author describes the countryside of his homeland, but the narration is burdened with a certain "artificial flavor," which Thoma, with his alert critical organ, sensed himself. Not long before young Kaspar's reluctant departure for school, he experiences the simple, but noble beauty of the South Bavarian landscape:

. . . there [I] was lying for hours behind the *Alm* on grassy hills from which one could see far out into the flatlands. The Isar River wound itself through the land like a vein of silver, [then] disappeared behind knolls and became visible again. Like the dark squares of a chessboard, the woods were lying below me: they narrowed, ran near villages in thin strips and powerfully roamed further away, leaving no room for anything else; at my right hand, towards the East, a few lakes sparkled up to me like precious stones, and behind them extended a large range of mountains which blended into the haze. Cloud shadows laid themselves on bright meadows, slipped hurriedly over church spires and houses, and behind them ran golden glitter from the sun, and drove them on.[8]

One cannot find more beautiful prose in all of Thoma's work. But masterful language alone does not make a novel, as Thoma himself knew all too well.

V   *Other Prose Works*

Between 1917 and 1920, Thoma wrote three other prose works. They attain the length one usually expects from novels, but none of them can withstand a comparison with his four major narratives. In *Altaich*, Thoma tells the cheerful little story of a village in Bavaria which wants to cash in on the new tourist boom. Unfortunately, the town is situated far from the main stream of traffic and offers very few attractions. An advertising campaign, conducted in several major newspapers, is successful in luring a number of guests from Austria, Switzerland and Prussia who arrive in search of a vacation paradise. For a while, the natives get along with the guests. But soon the citizens of Altaich begin to pay the price for the introduction of tourism. One of the newcomers, a man from Berlin, tries vigorously to bring some "order" into the local tourist business. In cooperation with some zealous citizens, he organizes a tourist association. Soon the townspeople begin to lose their enthusiasm, and tensions with the guests arise. Finally, the weather changes to rain, and the tourists pack their bags. After all the guests have left town, the citizens of Altaich resolve to return to their old way of life. The old "order" of *Gemütlichkeit* is restored, and that is the most important thing to the "Old Bavarians."

Thoma wanted *Altaich* to read "harmlessly and cozily."[9] This goal has undoubtedly been reached. But there is little else to distinguish this piece in any way. Most of the guests are caricatures, routinely drawn, as are nearly all of the natives. The whole product could pass as a newspaper novel in installments, but not much more. As Thoma once mentioned to Josef Hofmiller, the total impression of the town and its atmosphere is to be seen as being autobiographic. Traunstein, Thoma's home in his adolescent and early professional years, served as a model for the sleepy Altaich.[10] Only from that viewpoint is the novel of value to the reader. Judging it by literary criteria, *Altaich* ranks rather low within Thoma's prose. It was certainly not meant to become an epic work. Thoma considered writing it as a pastime, and that is all it turned out to be.

Münchnerinnen, the story of a housewife named Paula who falls into adulterous ways, was finished in 1919, a very sad year for Thoma and for Germany. Paula's husband, a corpulent, lazy grocer, notoriously neglects her in favor of his great investment and speculation plans which ultimately lead to disaster. Paula's lover is a university student who finally gives her up for a young girl his parents want him to marry. Paula is left the real loser.

Like *Altaich*, *Münchnerinnen* lacks the compactness and structure of a good novel. Originally, Thoma wanted to let Paula poison her husband unsuccessfully, but he later abandoned this idea.[11] He also changed the emphasis on the figures of the novel: initially, he talked about calling the work *Paula*, but while writing, decided on the title *Münchnerinnen*.[12] He must have realized that even Paula, who stands in the story's center, was not a substantial enough character to justify using her name as a title. And that is the main flaw of *Münchnerinnen*: the people in this novel cannot carry the story; they only serve as components of a "group picture." They are, at best, illustrations of the urban *Kleinbürger's* life at the end of the nineteenth century, as it existed in much of Europe. In this respect, *Münchnerinnen* finds itself on common ground with

Altaich, where the rural version of the petit bourgeois appears. But, in contrast to *Altaich*, *Münchnerinnen* remained a torso. Evidently, Thoma did not have the desire to finish it. To Maidi von Liebermann he wrote: "A novel like this Munich story, simply written off the cuff, I shall not write very soon again. To 'have to' invent is not pleasant. To describe something already invented is comfortable. But to turn around after six-hundred pages is impossible after all."[13]

Der Jagerloisl is set in Thoma's favorite territory, the Bavarian Alps. It should be remembered that most of Thoma's works either have little or no connection with the Alpine region of Bavaria. Almost all of the significant dramas and novels are set in the lowlands of Bavaria, particularly in the parts around Dachau. It is difficult to explain why in his writings Thoma favored the lowlands over the more spectacular mountains. It has been speculated that he wanted to save his homeland for greater works, which he still intended to write.[14] Whatever the reasons for his choice of scene, there are only a few pieces in which the *Oberland* plays a dominant role. One of these is *Kaspar Lorinser*; another is *Der Jagerloisl*, whose setting is the land around the Tegernsee, where an innocent little story unfolds, depicting the happenings of a summer in the life of Jagerloisl, a likeable young lad who takes his job as a forest ranger very seriously. He makes the mistake of falling in love with a pretty but flighty young girl from Berlin who is spending her summer vacation with her parents on the Tegernsee. Jagerloisl finds out in time that the wench only plays a flirting game with him, and his interest turns to a sturdy dairymaid whom he soon decides to marry.

Der Jagerloisl, although not to be compared to run-of-the-mill newspaper novels and short stories containing similar motifs, walks a thin line between art and *Kitsch*. Too many elements in the story remind the reader of the much-abused mountain romanticism, which raged through Germany in the early party of this century. The fad witnessed a spectacular revival after World War II, when tourism picked up again and finally destroyed everything genuinely romantic in the Alpine region. The beginning of tourism is reflected in *Der Jagerloisl*, which takes place at a time when the urban population discovered the charm and beauty of the *Oberland*. Never before had the rural way of life mixed on such a large scale with the customs and manners of the city dwellers. Making money from the tourists was the order of the day, and the tourist industry developed almost unbridled. In return, the mountain people had to sacrifice the tranquillity of their land, and also much of their identity.

Lola Montez is an unfinished novel about the famous dancer whose story exerted a strange fascination on Thoma. She appears twice in his prose works and once in his poetry. For the first time we hear about the notorious Irishwoman in *Andreas Vöst*, when the good Reverend Held tells about his student years in Munich, where he belonged to a small group of people who did not advocate that Lola Montez be banished from the city. According to the public opinion of that time, as the monarch's concubine and adviser, she was on the best way of ruining both King Ludwig I and all of Bavaria. Many loyal Bavarian subjects had been outraged by the king's decision to make his mistress the Countess of Landsfeld. Her increasing political influence at the court also worried many citizens. Last, but not least, it was the almost unthinkable audacity and directness with which Lola met the citizens of Munich which repulsed the Bavarians. In Munich, to have been known for defending Lola and her misdeeds in those days shortly before her banishment from the court and before the 1848 abdication of Ludwig I, must have been considered equal to having committed a crime. In *Lola Montez*, Thoma wants to make these turbulent times come alive. His hero is a young painter who gets involved in the Montez controversy against his will, when, while in a Munich tavern, he merely expresses his disgust about the self-righteousness of some people who cannot stop talking about the woman. He becomes known as a "Lolaist" and has to live under the threat of being censured by a court of honor formed by members of his artist's guild. Because of the denunciations of an evil competitor, he even stands to lose the friendship of the girl he secretly loves.

Unfortunately, Thoma could not finish this piece in which he wanted to tell much about prerevolutionary Bavaria in the form of memoirs written by an old painter. Again, the reader encounters the striking precision of Thoma's realistic style in this lovely little torso of no more than sixty-seven pages. In spite of the brevity of the story, Thoma manages to describe a great number of characters, all of whom in some way get mixed up in the Montez affair, including the famous painter, Carl Spitzweg, who takes on the role of a fatherly protector of the story's hero, helping him to regain his sweetheart's trust.

Thoma wrote numerous smaller works in prose, of which only a few will be mentioned in this chapter. In 1897, he published *Agricola*, a collection of stories portraying the unique phenomenon of the Bavarian peasant who dwells in the rural areas in small villages some of which are situated in the immediate vicinity of

Munich. As small and insignificant as these little hamlets and villages may seem to the passing traveler, the same cycle of human existence runs its course within their narrow boundaries and in their small-windowed houses and small churches as in the bustling cities. On closer inspection one finds that there are, nonetheless, distinguishing features. First of all, Thoma notices that the people in the rural districts have a unique attitude toward reality. Decadence or exuberant feelings are unknown to them. They see the world around them in a more pragmatic way than do the city dwellers; they are more honest in liking and disliking people; and they know that they have to fight a continuous struggle against the forces of nature which permanently threaten their existence in one way or another. The major stations in life are seen in a similarly practical light: before a young man decides to take a wife, he and his father will thoroughly investigate the suitability of the farm operation which he is to take over, and sometimes long negotiations will precede the conclusion of the marriage contract. Another prerequisite to the marriage is the "testing" of the bride, which the groom will undertake on the second floor while his father negotiates the details of the bride's dowry downstairs. All this happens without great gestures or emotions. The highlight of the wedding itself is a great feast for all the guests. Afterwards, the bride follows her husband, always a few steps behind him, since she is now his personal property. The peasant's life ends with the same quiet dignity in which it has been conducted. Although these people, who have so little use for sentiment, may seem unfeeling to the reader, their lives are full of joy and laughter, and of the deep emotions of sorrow and pain, even if never openly shown. What may seem to be brutality is more often merely frankness and honesty. This is the message Thoma wanted to convey in *Agricola*. Certainly he did not intend to downgrade the farmer and his way of life, as has been maintained. Thoma knew these people and admired their steadfastness and sound thinking, as well as their simple, down-to-earth morality.

CHAPTER 4

Humorous Prose and Satire

THE work for which Ludwig Thoma is best known in Germany is his *Lausbubengeschichten*, a sequence of hilarious little stories which appeared in 1905 with the subtitle, *Aus meiner Jugendzeit* (Stories from My Youth). As in Goethe's *Dichtung und Wahrheit*, not everything one reads in the *Lausbubengeschichten* is strictly autobiographical. However, the reader can very well picture Thoma as the central figure, the little fellow called Ludwig who terrorizes not only his enemies, but his mother and sister as well. Ludwig's first major scandal at school is caused by the discovery of a harmless love letter he had written to a young lady. Threatened with dismissal for breaking a school window, he saves his career as a student by covering up the truth to his "good" advantage. After his uncle helps him with his arithmetic homework and the teacher says that only a donkey could have done such stupid work, Ludwig gets into trouble with the teacher and his uncle, who blame him for incorrectly copying the uncle's "good" work. He gets the best of his special enemy, the school chaplain, by defacing a plaster statue of Saint Aloisius, the patron of students. During summer vacations, he causes an uproar among the guests when he cuts off the tail of their cat. To his great displeasure, his sister marries his former teacher, a real bore who constantly derides him for being a bad student and a soul beyond salvation; and when a baby arrives Ludwig earns the severe man's utter contempt when he refuses to recognize the onomatopoetic quality of the baby's squealing, which is admired by everyone else. When his first communion approaches, Ludwig decides to begin a new and better life, but soon gets into trouble again by blowing up another youngster's expensive toy steamboat with a charge of black powder. While riding on the train, returning home for vacations, he annoys people by throwing beer bottles out of the window and vomiting. But when he arrives, he again decides to become an orderly young man.

121

Ludwig's infallible sense for the hypocrisy of the adults around
him and his strong instinct for self-preservation are masterfully portrayed in the little story "Der Meineid" (The Perjury): having been
punished by the headmaster for beating up one of his classmates,
Ludwig decides to take revenge. He throws a stone into the headmaster's office on a Sunday, destroying one of his son's oil paintings. Suspecting Ludwig as the villain, the headmaster vigorously
tries to get a confession out of him, with the help of one of Ludwig's
teachers and the school chaplain:

Der Religionslehrer legte seine Hand auf meinen Kopf und tat recht
gütig, obwohl er mich sonst gar nicht leiden konnte.
"Du armer, verblendeter Junge," sagte er, "nun schütte dein Herz aus
und gestehe mir alles. Es wird dir wohl tun und dein Gewissen erleichtern."
"Und es wird deine Lage verbessern," sagte der Rektor.
"Ich war es doch gar nicht. Ich habe doch gar kein Fenster nicht
hineingeschmissen," sagte ich.
Der Religionslehrer sah jetzt sehr böse aus. Dann sagte er zum Rektor:
"Wir werden jetzt sofort Klarheit haben. Das Mittel hilft bestimmt." Er
führte mich zum Tische, vor die Kerzen hin, und sagte furchtbar feierlich:
"Nun frage ich dich vor diesen brennenden Lichtern. Du kennst die
schrecklichen Folgen des Meineides vom Religionsunterrichte. Ich frage
dich: Hast du den Stein hereingeworfen? Ja—oder nein?"
"Ich habe doch gar keinen Stein nicht hineingeschmissen," sagte ich.
"Antworte ja—oder nein, im Namen alles Heiligen!"
"Nein," sagte ich. Der Religionslehrer zuckte die Achseln und sagte:
"Nun war er es doch nicht. Der Schein trügt."
Dann schickte mich der Rektor fort.
Ich bin recht froh, dass ich gelogen habe und nichts eingestand, dass ich
am Sonntagabend den Stein hineinschmiss, wo ich wusste, dass das Bild
war. Denn ich hätte meine Lage gar nicht verbessert und wäre davongejagt
worden. Das sagte der Rektor bloss so. Aber ich bin nicht so dumm.[1]

The chaplain put his hand on my head and acted very benevolently,
although he could not stand me otherwise.
"You poor, misguided fellow," he said, "now go ahead and unload your
burdened heart and confess everything. It will make you feel better and
relieve your conscience."
"And it will improve the situation you are in," said the headmaster.
"But I was not the one who did it. I have not broke no window," I said.
The chaplain now had a very mean look on his face. Then he said to the
headmaster: "We will know the truth right away. That remedy will help for
sure." He led me to the table in front of the candles, and said in a terribly
solemn voice: "Now I ask you before these burning lights. You know the

terrible consequences of committing perjury, from studying the Scriptures. I ask you: Have you thrown the stone into the room? Yes or no?"

"I haven't thrown in no stone," I said.

"Answer yes or no, in the name of everything sacred!"

"No," I said. The chaplain shrugged his shoulders and said: "He was not the one after all. Appearances are deceptive."

Then the headmaster told me to leave.

I am very glad that I have lied and not confessed everything about throwing the stone into the office on Sunday, knowing that the picture was there. Because I would certainly not have improved my position at all, and I would have been expelled. The headmaster only said I would not be, without meaning it. But I am not that stupid.

Ludwig is by no means an irreligious monster. Knowing, however, that the solemnity of a sacred oath is not to be misused at such a trivial occasion, and being certain of his dismissal from school had he confessed the deed, he decides to tell a lie, thereby beating the mendacious adults at their own game.

Certainly some of Ludwig's pranks may seem to be rather cruel. However, one cannot help but sympathize with the young villain as he exposes the hypocrisy of the adults around him through his naughtiness and "straightforward dishonesty." Any spirited young lad would surely like to join the ornery youth in his wild adventures, and one might add, not only lads young in years.

In 1906, Thoma decided to write a sequence to the *Lausbubengeschichten* under the title *Tante Frieda* (Aunt Frieda). The heroine of the first little story in this new collection is actually one of Thoma's own aunts, a sister of his father, who lived as an old spinster in Munich. Thoma started to write *Tante Frieda* with the intention of inventing some new and even funnier adventures for the little rascal, Ludwig, to get involved in. But as it happens with many second attempts along similar lines, *Tante Frieda* did not turn out to be as fresh and lively in spirit as the original. However, it is still a distinct pleasure to follow Ludwig's adventures surrounding a visit by his peevish old aunt, who seems to take pleasure in behaving as tactlessly as possible, especially toward Ludwig's mother. Her nasty remarks about the baldness of Ludwig's sister's fiancé upset the young girl, who fears he is being driven away, until Ludwig's effective countermeasures promptly drive Tante Frieda herself to an early departure: Tante Frieda's pet parrot, Ludwig's special enemy from the beginning, is nearly blown to pieces by a charge of gunpowder the boy puts in its cage.

Ludwig's cousin, Cora, an exotic young beauty from India, causes an uproar in the small town when not only young fellows like Ludwig's friend, Franz, but also older gentlemen like Ludwig's uncle suddenly have eyes only for her. Ludwig, who likes being the center of attention, finds the new distraction uninteresting, to say the least, and manages to stay on top of the situation by perpetrating one misdeed after the other until his mother finally sends him to stay with a retired army captain and his wife, in hopes that they can straighten him out. But it does not take Ludwig long to find out that Mr. Semmelmaier's authority is not genuine, since he has to shut up when his wife talks. When Ludwig's mother sends him three marks, he and his friend Max spend the money on eggs to throw at people. Ludwig hits a nasty newspaper salesman with an egg, and is reported to Semmelmaier, who promptly claims that Ludwig stole thirty eggs from his wife's kitchen, for which he will charge Ludwig's mother. Incensed over the injustice, Ludwig decides to buy a toy rocket with which he will shell Semmelmaier's bedroom.

Without exaggeration, it can be said that the popularity of both the *Lausbubengeschichten* and *Tante Frieda* made the name of Ludwig Thoma a household word in Germany. With these two books, Thoma reached beyond the intelligentsia to an audience which usually shows no great interest in literature. The two stories are written in a style which a youngster of no more than twelve years would use in his diary. Grammar and syntax purposely show deficiencies that would be typical for an adolescent writer. An additional attraction for readers of the original edition were Olaf Gulbransson's pertinent illustrations, each one masterfully illustrating little Ludwig's incorrigible insolence. If Thomas Mann's secret desire was to be Felix Krull, Thoma's second identity is to be found in naughty Ludwig.

During the year 1908, right in the middle of several *Simplicissimus* battles, Thoma wrote the *Briefwechsel eines bayerischen Landtagsabgeordneten* (Correspondence of a Bavarian Deputy). Josef Filser, a farmer from the small town of Mingharting, is elected deputy of his rural district. He reports about the business of "governing," and about life in Munich in general, in a sequence of letters to his wife, to several friends, and to the parish priest who was instrumental in getting him elected. In his own naive manner, he explains to his readers how the Parliament under the leadership of the Center party, which is dominated by Catholic clergymen, intimidates the "big shots" (the cabinet ministers), and how wonderful it is to be able to let the powerful bureaucrats know what little they can do against the Center party, whose deputies are mainly farmers and priests:

Um zehn Uhr get die Bolidik an und mir gehen in das Barlamend hinein in den Sahl. Auf der einen Seit und in der Mitt sizen mir und machen beinah alles voll, denn mir sind die Mehreren, dan komen die lüberalen freimaurer und dan komen die Sozi. Oben auf siezt der Orterer und geibt Obacht auf ins, das nichts bassiert und bal einer die fotzen recht aufreist, schwengelt er mit seiner Glocken.

Es gibt sogenante Generalredner und Schpezialredner. Die Generalredner sind der Daller und der Pichler, weil sie es am besten wiesen und immer dran komen.

Liber Freind, Du hast mir geschriben, ich soll es im Barlamend forbringen, das Dich der Schandarm aufgeschrieben hat, weils Du an einen öffendlichen Weg Deine Notdurft gemacht hast.

Liber Freind, ich bringe es schon for, aber der Pichler hat gesagt, das gehört ins Minisderium des Innern, aber jetzt hamm wir die Justits in der Arbeit. Ich glaube schon, das mir dem Schandarm eine Suppen einbrocken und das ihm der Minisder einen Deuter gibt, denn sie ziddern schon, wenn mir blos mit die Augn blinseln.

Es ist schad, das die Nortdurft nicht zum Kuldusbidschö geheert, denn er ist inser bester Freind und zidderd noch mehrer, wie die andern.

Überhaupts, liber Schpezi, wen Due wiesen thetest, was fir einen Reschpekt die Grosskobfeden for uns haben, mechtest Du schaugn und keine Angst nicht mer haben zwegn Deiner Notdurft.[2]

At ten o'clock politics start and we all walk into the Hall of Parliament. We sit on the one side and in the middle, and fill up almost everything, because we are the majority. Then there are the liberal Masons and then there are the Sozis. Orterer sits above everyone and as soon as somebody opens his mouth too much, he rings the bell.

There are so-called general speakers and special speakers. The general speakers are Daller and Pichler, because they know it all and it is always their turn to speak.

My dear friend, you have written that I should inform the Parliament about your having been arrested by a policeman because you defecated on a public road. My dear friend, I will indeed inform the Parliament, but Mr. Pichler said that it is a matter concerning the Department of the Interior, but we are right now deliberating on the Department of Justice. I am sure that we will teach that policeman a lesson and that the minister will reprimand him, because they [the ministers] already tremble when we just blink our eyes.

It is a pity that defecating in public does not pertain to the budget of the

Department of Education and Culture, because he [the minister] is our best friend and he trembles even more than the others.

Anyway, old buddy, if you only knew the respect these bigwigs show for us, you would not be afraid any more about your defecation.

Filser also reports about the temptations of the big city and how he got involved with a loose woman, was beaten up, robbed, and thrown out of an establishment. He lets his audience know that the evil wench even had the audacity to blackmail him by threatening to write to his wife, telling her that he had fathered her baby. After having done penance for his sins, Filser concludes his reports with some thoughts about religion, science, the arts, and finally about the position of Bavaria vis-à-vis foreign countries, mainly Prussia.

In the second part of the *Briefwechsel*, which appeared in 1912 under the title *Jozef Filsers Briefwexel, Zweites Buch*, the deputy continues his naive-satirical account of life in Parliament, but now speaking as an expert. Triumphantly, he reports the Center party's latest victory, the banning of the *Simplicissimus* from the Bavarian railroad. Already in his next epistle he expresses his concern about coming home to Mingharting at Christmas because he fears that his constituency will make him responsible for the rising beer prices. At home, he indeed gets beaten unconscious by the enraged citizens, who categorically reject his attempts to explain the reasons for the new beer prices. Back in Munich, troublesome news reaches him from home. His wife has gotten into a fight with the parish priest's cook, a resolute woman who bosses everybody around. The priest, Filser's former mentor, blames the fight on the deputy, calling him a bad Catholic, and ordering him to resign from his elected office. In the meantime, Parliament is dissolved because of severe differences with the executive branch, and entirely against his will Filser has to return to Mingharting. But he uses his vacation to good advantage: in a letter to the archbishop, he complains about the meanness of the parish priest, who is trying to force him to resign from his office as deputy. He tells the archbishop about an illicit affair between the cook and the chaplain whom the priest proposes to have replace Filser in Parliament. In a second letter, Filser can already report that the parish priest has suffered a stroke and is no longer among the living. Nothing now stands in the way of Filser's reelection to the new Parliament. Reelected and back in Munich, he jubilantly describes the revenge which the Center party is taking on the unruly, liberal cabinet. To the new parish priest of Mingharting he jovially extends his congratulations, adding that the papal order banning female cooks from the parsonages would not apply to Bavaria, according to the results of the investigation Filser himself had undertaken on the priest's behalf. The second part of the *Filserbriefe* concludes on a vehemently anticlerical note directed at the leadership of the Center party, who finally wants to expel Filser from the Parliament, calling him a disgrace to all farmers in Bavaria.

The two volumes of the *Filserbriefe* are the most controversial of Thoma's works. Not only did they cause innumerable and vigorous reactions at the time of their publication, but they also are a cause for polarization among contemporary critics. Whereas some find the *Filserbriefe* to be an unnecessary satirical bombardment of an enemy who does not even deserve an attack in a literary form, others find them amusing and ingeniously satirical.[3] If one wants to judge the *Filserbriefe* fairly, one has to search for a middle ground between condemnation and euphoric praise. These fictitious letters penned by one of Thoma's most beloved characters are exceedingly funny in their own, peculiar way, because Thoma definitely succeeded in making us see the political world through the eyes of a Dachau farmer. A man like Filser may appear naive and even stupid to an "enlightened" city dweller of the twentieth century who might be tempted to judge the man by his own standards. Nevertheless, he will discover that much of what Filser reports in his letters has a disarming effect on the hostile reader, because of its blatant honesty and crude realism. Filser himself is fully aware of his precarious position: after he is elected, having been put on the ballot by his parish priest, who sees in him a stupid but willing instrument, Filser has to face the contempt of his political comrades-in-arms, the carnal temptations of the big city, blackmail from his "friends" at home, the threats of his wife, and finally, the vicious attacks of his former mentor, the parish priest. Burdened with pressures and intimidations from all sides, Filser weathers these storms rather well. He remains a deputy in spite of all the intrigues his enemies are spinning against him. The main target of Thoma's stirring satire is the Bavarian Center party, which ruled Parliament from 1899 on and was almost entirely dominated by clergymen. In Thoma's view, the Center party's leaders not only terrorized the government bureaucracy and railroaded the opposition, but they also ruled their own party's representatives with an iron hand, always telling them how to vote, and otherwise treating them with flagrant disrespect. The language in which Filser writes his letters is that of his home region right down to the faulty phonemic spelling, vocabulary, and syntax. Today's reader, at a healthy distance from Bavarian politics of the turn of the century, will not be bothered by the humiliating caricatures of then-contemporary politicians. The Center party's chairman, Orterer, for instance, appears as an absolute idiot. Having lost their topicality, the *Filserbriefe* have gained in literary value. One can see them now as a humorous view of a political era which is long past. They were conceived by an ingenious satirist who wrote with a very sharp pen. It should not be forgotten that Thoma intended the *Filserbriefe* to be vicious and aggressive in their purpose of exposing the political opponent. Fifteen years after Thoma had created his secret weapon, Josef Fisler, he deeply regretted the way in which he had unleashed him.

During his lifetime, Ludwig Thoma was known mainly for his piercing satires. Although he had a considerable reputation as a playwright even before World War I, in Bavaria people either loved or hated him for his monthly contributions, between 1897 and 1914, to the *Simplicissimus*, consisting of small prose pieces or poems.

In Thoma's *Gesammelte Werke*, the prose satires are subdivided into several subjects.[4] In the first category, described by the motto *Daheim und bei den andern* (At Home with Elsewhere), facets of everyday life in Bavaria, Austria, and Prussia are portrayed with merciless sarcasm. In "Auf der Elektrischen" (On the Streetcar), Thoma describes a scene in which everything said by a man who looks and sounds like a Prussian is interpreted by the other passengers as an insult to them, even when he is agreeing with them.

"Der Münchner im Himmel" (A Man from Munich in Heaven) quickly became popular. In it, a Munich porter called Hingerl suddenly dies and goes to heaven, where he is supposed to take part in constant hallelujah-singing and manna-eating. When he refuses to do this, God has mercy on the poor man and sends him back to Munich to deliver divine inspirations to the Minister of Culture. But upon returning to the city, Hingerl follows his old habit and makes a stop at the *Hofbräuhaus*. He is still sitting there today, and the Minister has yet to receive the divine inspirations.[5]

"Amalie Mettenleitner" is a bitter satire on the women's movement.[6] In the first paragraph, Thoma defines this sociological phenomenon as "a movement of those unmarried females who do not have anything better to do. It originates from the *Weltschmerz* of a Grete who has no Hans, and is aimed at the 'right of the woman' which begins where the 'right of the man' ends." Amalie Mettenleitner is an unattractive, middle-aged spinster who becomes an enthusiastic follower of the movement. Soon she is known among her peers as a notorious man-hater. She frequently unloads her hatred against the other sex in public speeches, and once in the middle of such a fiery speech she claims that the sight of a pair of men's trousers nauseates her. One evening she finds flowers and a small card from an admirer on her table. The admirer turns out to be one of her neighbors, an ugly little man with a head too big for his size. The two begin to see each other regularly, and after one year Amalie gives birth to a child, much to the dismay of her dumbfounded sisters in the woman's movement. When the president of the movement reminds Amalie of her statement that the sight of men's trousers nauseated her, Amalie replies in tears: "Yes, but, you know, *at that time* he did not wear any trousers."

Thoma satirizes the snobbishness of the average German tourist in Italy in "Die Familie in Italien" (The Family in Italy). A mother and daughter race from one museum to another, following the instructions in the Baedeker travel guide, while the father seems only interested in thoughts about the good German breakfast he will have when finally at home again. In the end, the mother and daughter, who had initially scolded the father for his narrow-mindedness, even agree with him.

A very similar picture of a family from the German North is presented in "Käsebiers Italienreise" (Käsebiers' Italian Journey). Thoma considered German tourists abroad to be an obnoxious tribe, especially those from north of the Main River. He himself had had ample opportunity to observe their overbearing behavior, their inclination to brag, and their habit of patronizing the natives.

A noteworthy account of the earlier days of newspaper reporting is to be found in "Der Interviewer." During a stay in Vienna, where one of his plays is being performed, an author grants an interview to an aggressive reporter who, as it turns out, has entirely preconceived ideas about the author. Since the author is known as a satirist who frequently says derogatory things about the government, the reporter expects such *bon mots* during the interview, but is disappointed. He leaves, convinced that no one will believe his account of the interview if he merely reports that he found the author in a sparkling mood, indulging himself, as usual, in satirical remarks about various subjects. Since there is nothing controversial to write, because the satirist had nothing controversial to say, the reporter frets that his public will surely think that he had made up lies about the interview.

In "Eine psychologische Studie" (A Psychological Study), a

bridegroom first seeks professional advice in sexual matters from a professor of zoology, but finally consults an encyclopedia to find out what he needs to know. Once informed, he promptly succeeds in producing a male offspring for the fatherland.

Thoma again picks up his favorite theme of the Bavarian "original" in heaven in "Der Postsekretär im Himmel" (The Postal Clerk in Heaven). Martin Angermayer, a post-office clerk from Munich, has a dream in which he dies and is subsequently thrown out of heaven by two rude Bavarian angels. To his surprise and joy, he wakes up to find himself lying in the dirty snow of a Munich street, very much alive but only vaguely able to recall his apparently having been tossed out of a *Brauhaus*.

Another category of satires bears the title *Von Rechts wegen* (By Dint of the Law). The individual pieces deal with shortcomings and abuses in the law profession, a subject Thoma knew rather well since he had been a lawyer. "Assessor Karlchen," for instance, caused a regular uproar among Germany's lawyers. A police jurist, Karlchen pays one of his subordinates, a policeman on the beat, to prove the deliquency of a certain lady of the town suspected of being a prostitute. The obliging policeman is so thorough in his investigation that he succeeds in making the vivacious lady pregnant. After she is kicked out of town by Karlchen, a request for alimony arrives in his office. He has no choice but to pay it out of his own salary in order to keep the affair from becoming known. A more biting satire on the overzealousness of an official is hardly possible. One can easily understand that bureaucrats all over Germany resented it that someone in Munich was publishing one gloss after another on the stupidity of government officials and clergymen. It must have been a great pleasure for them to see the much-feared mocker sitting in Stadelheim prison for six weeks during the autumn of 1906.

Written in the same spirit, and equally demolishing to a jurist, is "Der Einser" (meaning "the one who received an 'A' in his bar examination"). Thoma was bothered by this kind of classification, maintaining that mere knowledge of articles of law does not make a good lawyer. In "Der Einser," one of the "A" graduates is confronted with a young widow who wants to adopt a little girl. The young lawyer puts the lady through an ordeal of questioning before starting to process the matter. At the end of the interrogation, the little child hands him a small bouquet of flowers to express her gratitude. Now his embarrassment is complete, because these flowers could be interpreted as a bribe. In a lengthy memorandum to his superior he asks for guidance. The flowers, representing the *corpus delicti*, end up as an exhibit in a folder, where they quickly wilt.

Thoma's great aversion to this type of narrow-minded and humorless jurist shows up in several other satires. "Der Vertrag" (The Contract) begins with the sentence: "The Royal State Official, Alois Eschenberger, was a good jurist and otherwise, also of moderate intellect."[7] Naturally, Eschenberger belongs to the category of lawyers who received an "A" in the bar examinations, and therefore has license to commit any foolishness he wants to. As long as he lives, everything he does must be recorded in a legal contract. When his housekeeper suggests that the bed linens be replaced, he agrees to sell the old sheets to a pawnbroker. Of course, the transaction has to be concluded by the signing of a meticulously drawn-up contract. The little pawnbroker is at first reluctant to get involved in such a ridiculous formality over a few sheets, but finally signs the legal document and leaves with the bundle of sheets. Soon the housekeeper discovers that there has been a mixup. Instead of taking the old sheets, the pawnbroker mistakenly took along the bundle containing the new bed linens. When he is urgently asked to return the bundle, he laughingly refuses. He is, after all, in possession of a legal paper certifying that the transaction took place in an orderly fashion.

Not quite so offending to the legal profession is "Unser guter, alter Herzog Karl" (Our Good, Old Duke Karl). A hobo manages to spend sixteen winters in a warm prison cell by deliberately committing a *lèse majestè* in public, as soon as the autumn nights begin to be chilly. He merely calls Duke Karl a "blockhead" and gets himself arrested and convicted every time, just as he intends. When the lawmakers begin to consider easing the provisions on *lèse majestè*, the little hobo faces the loss of his winter quarter.

The first story under the heading of *Im Dienst der Musen* (In the Service of the Muses), entitled "Das Volkslied," tells about the plan of a country lawyer to put together a collection of *Volkslieder*. He takes the enterprise most seriously because he sees it as a service to his fatherland. Since he himself is unfamiliar with the old songs he is searching for, he decides to get the help of a native informant whom he soon finds in the person of one of his farmer clients. The old farmer agrees to listen to the young locals sing on the weekend and to write down the songs they sing in their drunkenness, for

which the lawyer promises to pay a small stipend. After a few weeks
the farmer presents the lawyer with a greasy little notebook containing, in faulty spelling and horrible handwriting, the texts of
such songs as "Die Wacht am Rhein," "Ich hatte einen
Kameraden," "Oh du lieber Augustin," and other well-known
songs, not one of them a genuine folksong. Utterly discouraged and
four marks lighter, the country lawyer abandons his plan for the
collection. In this little story, Thoma again wants to demonstrate
the complete helpnessness of the narrow-minded and arrogant jurist
up against a sly Bavarian peasant.

Strongly influenced by personal experience is the rather lengthy
satire "Heimkehr" (Return), which tells about the peculiar education a young dramatist obtains on the occasion of the performance
of his play on the Berlin stage. Since he is a native of Tübingen, the
Berlin public looks on him as a writer from the provinces. Following
the performance, he meets the critics in a restaurant. They make
very complimentary remarks about his talent, giving him the impression that he has made it in the big theater world of the
metropolis. During that night he has a mysterious dream in which a
mythical figure, the Ghost of Lake Constance, threatens to beat him
with an oar if he should stay in Berlin any longer. The author wakes
up scared and confused, and only begins to understand the meaning
of the dream after reading the morning paper: the same critics who
had praised him the night before either patronize him in their
reviews or downright reject his play. The author draws the consequences immediately and leaves the city on the next express train.

Quite vulgar, but irresistible in its comicality, is "Die unter-
brochene Berta" (The Interrupted Berta). An overzealous chaplain
whose ambition it is to force the people of his town to perform a
sentimental religious drama against their will, falls victim to his own
effort. A cynical old peg-legged farmer from the nearby countryside
gets the best seat in the balcony for the performance. He proceeds
to transform the sentimental mood of the viewers into an orgy of
laughter, making a continuation of the performance impossible, by
producing a loud and lengthy indecent noise at the most moving
moment in the plot.

In "Der Krieg in China" (The War in China), a young woman
who is in search of literary motifs for a novel she is planning to
write, accompanies the author on a walk to the train station, where
troops are being shipped to China.[8] The author makes observations
about each passing soldier, describing, with tongue in cheek, how

each one of them—whose individual circumstances he professes to know personally—would be a suitable character for a sentimental novel. After leaving the station, still not realizing that the author has actually been pulling her leg, the would-be writer rushes home to begin writing her novel.

Very amusing little satires are to be found in the last category, entitled *Von Thron, Altar und Revolution* (About Throne, Altar and Revolution). In "Woldemar," a young government official sits alone on Christmas Eve in a Berlin café reading sentimental stories. He is overcome by a desire to have a home with a wife and blond-haired youngsters. When tears begin to fill his eyes, he suddenly remembers that he has been invited to spend Christmas Eve at the home of a Berlin merchant who has a young unmarried daughter. Within half an hour, he is holding the rich man's daughter in his arms.

Among several satirical pieces treating such subjects as the nobility with its antiquated customs, and the persecution of the press, one finds "Missionspredigt des P. Josephus gegen den Sport" (Mission Sermon of Father Joseph against Sports), in which a Catholic priest preaches against the newly imported, bad habit called "sports." In Bavarian dialect, he demonstrates the immoral influence of sports on people's souls, especially on women's.

Probably one of the best satires Thoma wrote is "Der Krieg. Ein Schulaufsatz" (The War: A Composition Exercise). Barely two pages long, it is written in the form of a high-school student's composition. It starts with a disarming definition of war: "War (bellum) is a situation, in which two or more nations test each other. It has been known since earliest times, and because it appears so often in the Bible one calls it sacred." The composition proceeds in simple, naive language, expressing all the cruelty and hypocrisy surrounding the phenomenon of war, and ends with the comical assessment: "All of those who have taken part in a war receive round medals which clank when the owner goes for a walk with them. Many also get rheumatism and become janitors at the *Gymnasium*, as ours did. And so also war has its benefits and fertilizes everything."[9]

In the last prose satire, entitled "Bildung und Fortschritt" (Education and Progress), a young girl of rural background has discovered that in the city one does not even need to have a job in order to enjoy life. She writes a letter to a girl friend in her hometown, who is working in the country as a servant, with the intention of enticing her to join her. In the letter she describes the wonderful new advantages of life in the city, where one is not exploited by capitalists, but can go to the movie theater in the middle of the afternoon every day, since the "gallants'" that one meets will support one for a while, making work unnecessary. In this satire, Thoma aims at the depressing circumstances prevailing in large German cities at the end of World War I, when the black market was thriving and when the cinema came into being. Radical socialism also began to have significant influence on the broad masses, a situation Thoma deplored and frequently blamed on the political leaders during these years of irresponsible politics and cheap demagogy.

Most of Thoma's lyric poems fall under the heading of satire, and were written mainly for publication in the *Simplicissimus*. In the edition of 1968, they are subdivided according to themes. Among the first of these subchapters, bearing the title *Im Lauf des Jahres* (In the Course of the Year), about a dozen poems may be considered satires. The subjects dealt with include, among others, a New Year's celebration at the home of a pastor who is so interested in the alcoholic punch being prepared by his wife that he can hardly concentrate on the sermon he is giving to his guests; the advent of the spring season, awakening a variety of human instincts; holidays in the country, when husbands play cards in order to escape the endless gossiping of their wives; and other erotic subjects. One finds only a few serious lyric pieces among this set, most of them of litttle significance.

Within the second subchapter of satiric lyric poetry, *Moritaten und Balladen* (Broadsides and Ballads), Eros is the main theme around which the individual poems gravitate. The characters portrayed include a puritanic high-school teacher who is a good family man but forgets his own strict moral principles during one night in Schwabing; an aging lover who is only good enough for paying the restaurant bill; the daughter of a patrician family in Hamburg who is forced to marry a jobless bum from the Balkans because he made her pregnant while she was an art student in Munich; a waitress who loses her innocence to an artist who had borrowed money from her; a bourgeois family whose members get involved in amorous adventures during the Carnival season; a Protestant pastor who, while preaching morals to the people, is busy breeding like a rabbit with his wife (a favorite theme of Thoma's, who sees the married clergyman as a *contradictio per se*). In this set, Thoma also satirizes dance as an erotic stimulant, especially the Tango, which he favors least of all since only thin women can dance it; and, according to Thoma, men prefer ladies who are a little corpulent. Finally, he has a little fun with the birth of a prince to the House of Hohenzollern, an event which fills all Prussian hearts with joy, but which is of little interest to the Bavarians.

The next category among the satiric poems is entitled *Politisch Lied* (Political Song). Unfortunately, the limits of the current study do not leave enough room for a discussion of the numerous poems in this section. For almost a quarter of a century, Thoma was one of the most alert and intelligent watchers of German politics. The main targets of his biting satires, already known to the reader from earlier chapters, focus on the Bavarian Center party and its domination by clergymen; the bureaucracy of the Protestant churches; the often ridiculous public behavior of Wilhelm II; individuals in national politics, like Prince von Bülow (1849-1929), who held the office of *Reichskanzler* between 1900 and 1909, and his successor, Theobald von Bethmann-Hollweg (1856-1921), who left office in 1917; the British war in South Africa against the Boers (1899-1902), and the atrocities committed by the British army in this war, as well as the senselessness of war in general; Edward VII of England; Czar Nicholas of Russia; and finally, the political situation in Europe, which Thoma compares to an ailing mother, drifting toward World War I.

Thoma did not write any satirical poems of political content after 1914. The time, with its most serious and saddening events, did not seem fit for this type of criticism.

The subjects treated in *So war's einmal* (That's How It Once Was) include Bismarck and the way he was dismissed; foreign potentates visiting Berlin; the memorial days in honor of his majesty, with their pomp and strange comicality; the National Liberal party; big industry; the police; the duel as an institution; the government bureaucracy; price increases; and academic freedom. If one were to continue the list of topics treated by Thoma in his satires, one would discover that over the years he covered almost all facets of life. Two poems within this chapter became widely known and even enjoyed a peculiar kind of fame. The first was "Assessorchen," which deals with a narrow-minded government attorney who is in charge of press censorship.[10] The poem was ill-received by the representatives of the government, and it helped in branding Thoma a declared enemy of the authorities. The second poem, "An die Sittlichkeitskonferenz zu Magdeburg" (To the

Morals Convention in Magdeburg), makes reference to the attempts of the morals societies, who are meeting in Magdeburg, to have Thoma brought to trial and imprisoned because of the "immorality" of some of his satiric poems. It makes fun of the purpose of the societies by telling them that they would not be able to prevent either men or animals from making love to each other. The poem closes with these two lines: "Halläh! and Lujah! Bäh! and Muh! The calves also don't get born by themselves."[11] This came very close to being a flagrant sacrilege, as far as the morals societies were concerned, and they countered by bringing the matter to court.

Only two poems in the last chapter of poems, *Krieg und Soldaten* (War and Soldiers), can be called satires. "Friede" (Peace) describes the euphoric mood following a victorious battle. The monarchs are feasting and toasting while the dead soldiers quietly dream away beneath the battlefields.[12] The second, "Kanonenfutter" (Cannon Fodder) consists of only four lines: "Behind the walls, behind the stacks, lies your fatherland. You fight for it, you die, yet you have never known it."[13]

In complete contrast to this negative assessment of war, stands the poem "1. August 1914," in which the author witnesses the people in the countryside as they learn about the outbreak of World War I. He observes their patriotic reactions and readiness to defend their country.[14]

There is no trace of satire or sarcasm to be found among the remaining poems, which deal with scenes from the front, Christmas Eve on the battlefields in France, the suffering of East Prussia during the war. Finally, there is a touching poem written for the dedication in 1921 of a chapel in Unterbachern memorializing the war dead.

Other poems in this group dealing with soldiers and the military in general are mostly written in a jovial mood. The themes are the departure of the soldier from his loved one, his thoughts about his girl at home, and the soldier's pride in his military unit, as exemplified in "Der bayerische Chevauleger" (The Bavarian Cavalryman) and in "Der Leiber" (The Soldier in the House Regiment).[15]

CHAPTER 5

Conclusion

L UDWIG Thoma died more than half a century ago, shortly after
the end of World War I, which at that time was seen as the
greatest catastrophe mankind had ever gone through. Today, more
than thirty years after an even more devastating global war, his
work seems to have gained in stature, not only because it has been
freed from the controversies of its own time, but because of its unique character, its truth, honesty, and depth, and its old-Bavarian
vitality and humor. As the past half century has afforded us the opportunity to reassess his literary legacy, the distance it has provided
also enables us to see Thoma, the man and the author, in a more
objective light.

Thoma was a robust, good-natured man of medium build, with a
large head resting on heavy shoulders, a broad face with a little
moustache and a small turned-up nose. All in all, he was a typical
Bavarian figure, as they are frequently found in the areas between
the Danube and the Alpine regions of Austria. The clothes he
favored suited his physique perfectly: in most of the photographs
we have of him, he is seen wearing a heavy, coarse, woollen jacket,
leather knee breeches, knee socks, and heavy mountain shoes or
boots. Thoma detested dressing in a formal suit or tuxedo, a point of
contention with his wife, Marion, already in the early stage of their
short marriage. He was a "down home" Bavarian, averse to formalities and social pressures, fond of good eating, a glass of beer,
strong coffee, and, most of all, a pipe filled with Latakia tobacco.

The well-known Bavarian proverb, "I want my royal Bavarian
peace," may be applied to Thoma in its full meaning. In his house
on the "Tuften" he had found this special kind of serenity and
tranquillity. Indeed, the house became the focal point in his life, especially after the separation from Marion, an event that left it emp-
tier but quieter than it had been during her presence. Thoma suffered heavily under Marion's desire to have parties with the house

full of people all the time. He felt lonely and out of place during the loud and shallow gatherings. As late as 1919, he remarked in a letter to Maidi von Liebermann: "Horrible were the . . . days of 1908 - 1909 - 1910. . . . Everything [was so] mendacious and treacherous. All the jolliness [was so] artificial. I was ill-humored and the fifth wheel on the cart, repelled and mad about the bad taste. . . ."[1] For Thoma the house was a refuge from the outside world, a castle against a stormy sky. And it was built as solidly as a castle, with only the best materials available used in its construction. The striking resemblance between the house on the "Tuften" and the ranger house in the Vorderriss provides clear evidence that it was Thoma's intention to recreate his boyhood home and thereby regain a measure of the happiness of former times. Whether or not the house provided the desired nostalgic link with the past, it did not assure his happiness. Within two years after moving into the "Tuften," Thoma's marriage ended and he lost his three closest friends and colleagues—Rudolf Wilke, Albert Langen, and Ferdinand von Reznicek. The friendship of these men, who had been Thoma's trusted comrades-in-arms during the stormiest years of the *Simplicissimus*, and whom death had taken with such cruel suddenness, was irreplaceable. After 1909, Thoma was increasingly alone. After his good friend Ignatius Taschner followed the others in death in November 1913, Thoma felt that an epoch had ended. He had reached the zenith of his creative power; all of his major stage plays had already been written. He began to feel that he, too, was in the sunset of his years. Intensifying his darkened mood were the sufferings he witnessed during the war years. The prospect of finally marrying Maidi yon Liebermann provided the only bright light of these years. This hope gave his life meaning and purpose, and provided the energy to undertake prose work as enormous as *Der Ruepp* and as ambitious as *Kaspar Lorinser*. Deep tragedy lies over the last ten years of Thoma's life: he lost the friends he had valued; he hoped in vain for the woman he wanted to marry; he believed himself to have lost the fatherland he loved through Germany's defeat; and he felt his physical strength dwindling.

Even in these gloomy years, writing remained the central purpose of Thoma's existence. And working on a new prose piece or a play was never a painful exercise. For Thoma, writing about people and their fates also meant sharing their adventures and problems. Although this often led to a deep involvement in the particular project he happened to be working on, he knew when to divert his attention if it became too narrowly focused on the events in the story or drama. In such a case, he would read historical studies by Heinrich von Treitschke or Theodor Mommsen, which had nothing whatever to do with the fortune of the Bavarian peasants about whom he might have been writing. This escape enabled Thoma to gain a certain distance, necessary for the successful completion of the work.

The literary examples on which Thoma trained himself, by reading intensive studies of their style and structure, were authors like Gottfried Keller, Wilhelm Raabe, and Theodor Fontane, who became his declared favorite among the German prose authors. He admired the almost unmatched clarity, the noble simplicity and transparency of style in Fontane's *Effi Briest*. Fontane's works, as well as the later works of Goethe, instilled in Thoma the desire to describe real life sovereignly, as it is, free of psychoanalytical explications, which he deeply abhorred. In his mature years, Thoma began to develop a disliking for the so-called "radicals" in nineteenth-century German literature. In reference to Georg Büchner, he makes a comparison to music: ". . . You know, such things as *Wozzek* [Woyzeck] et cetera are quite interesting, but they are not gratifying. That is like listening to a rehearsal conducted by a gifted band director who is showing off, instead of hearing Beethoven or your beloved Brahms."[2] The clarity and simple noblesse of classical music, by composers such as Mozart and Beethoven, fascinated Thoma as much as did Goethe's prose. For him, simplicity meant realism, and realism, truth.

Although Thoma was a very industrious writer, he did not stick to his "literary office hours," as Thomas Mann did so faithfully. This would have been contrary to Thoma's nature. He was a choleric character, driven by enthusiasm and by strong feelings about a subject. Emotions also guided Thoma in his political views and convictions, and he was never ashamed of them. How, indeed, could one be cold and rational about one's fatherland? One has to love it, or one is not human. His choleric disposition also determined his way of writing. As soon as he had decided on a theme, he started to write with great enthusiasm. His imagination usually supplied him with enough raw materials to carry the story through to the conclusion. As soon as he had fully identified with the plot, he could finish a project in a very short time. Sometimes it was not even necessary for him to make corrections in the first draft, so perfectly was he able to formulate his thoughts. His extraordinary mastery of the language is striking. During the hectic weeks and months of creating, his fine sense of stylistic propriety never left him, not even at points when his emotional attachment to his figures might have carried him away. He never indulged in lengthy verbal excursions, nor did he engage in untimely monologues.

It happened quite frequently that Thoma started his stories or novels without knowing their outcome. Sometimes he had to stop in the middle of his work and debate with himself about what his hero should do next. These discussions were often carried over into his correspondence with Maidi von Liebermann or with other intimate friends. Occasionally he got tired of writing on a subject after several months. Then he would start one or even two new projects and continue working on three pieces concurrently. At other times, when he would be interrupted by an outside event, or his imagination would begin to fail him, he would stop working altogether for a few days, or even weeks, to go hunting or travel. When he was working on a peasant story, he frequently interrupted his work to travel to Dachau and surrounding areas to gather new inspiration. There he would see his beloved "old-Bavarian" farmers in their natural setting, and when he returned to his study on the "Tuften," the stream of narration again flowed richly. Seldom did his imagination fail him completely. Among the more substantial works only *Kaspar Lorinser* remained a torso.

Thoma treated dramatic plots somewhat differently. He hesitated to begin a play before the entire concept was laid out in his mind. The density of the dramatic form did not permit any surprises, since sudden turns would infringe on the homogeneity of the plot.

Most of Thoma's works are based on inspirations provided by real-life situations: a wedding in a country village, a train ride from Dachau to Munich, a newspaper article, a funeral, a fight in a country tavern, a trial in a district court, or the excitement of a deer hunt. All these events and the people involved in them appear almost miraculously authentic and original in Thoma's stories and dramatic plots. This peculiar and rare authenticity also reaches into the linguistic area. Both in Thoma's prose works and in his plays, the vocabulary and syntax of the dialect spoken around Dachau are authentically rendered, in near-perfect phonetic transcription. In other words, Thoma does not simply set a story in the rural environment. He recreates life in this special world of the Bavarian farmer, unique in its moral code (as in *Magdalena*), its conventions and habits, its rhythm of life, its convictions, and its language. It is entirely inappropriate to see Thoma's *Erster Klasse*, for instance, or some of the humoristic short stories, merely as examples of slapstick comedy. There is nothing contrived or synthetic in these works and their humor. They are real portraits of life; indeed they are life itself. Naturally, the same applies to Thoma's serious works. In "Sterben" (Dying), death is described with almost brutal realism, but at the same time the reader is deeply touched by the dignity with which it is accepted by the country people.[3] The same unsentimental realism is to be found in such works as *Andreas Vöst* and *Magdalena*.

Because of the piercing realism in his works, it is a mistake to connect Thoma in any way with the so-called *Heimatkunst* (regional art) of late nineteenth- and early twentieth-century literature, whose representatives have usually had very little association with realism. Products of *Heimatkunst* try to sentimentalize and glorify life in the country, thereby creating a totally false impression in the minds of their readers. In his prose, on the other hand, Thoma never openly glorifies or admires: his mission is to give a genuine account of life itself in an appropriate artistic manner.

It is quite difficult to determine Thoma's position in German literature using the conventional criteria of literary history. It can be stated, however, without entering into any controversy, that his models, i.e., Goethe, Keller, Fontane, and Raabe, have to a great extent helped him to forge his own prose style. This does not make him either a classicist or a realist in literary-historical terms. It may well be that it is Thoma's ability to stay out of the very intensive stylistic quarrels and developments of his own time which has made him ultimately timeless, and therefore classical, in the wider sense of the term.

As far as Thoma's literary significance within Bavaria is concerned, to say that Thoma has remained the uncontested favorite among the writers of this region, as popular today as at the time of his death, is a fair assessment. He made his way into the school books long ago, and his plays appear frequently on the Munich stages. Through the last decades, his countrymen have developed a rather special affinity for Thoma, regarding him as a patron saint of Bavarian writers. The almost legendary popularity which Thoma continues to enjoy half a century after his death was well expressed during the 1971 festivities celebrating the author on the fiftieth anniversary of his death.

Nationally, Thoma never has commanded the same high reputation that he enjoys in Bavaria. After the initial success of his comedies in Berlin, interest in his works has been rather limited in the northern regions of Germany, where he was never completely able to shed the image of a *Heimatdichter,* and where his novels and satires were treated as mere products of a fertile Bavarian mind, rather than as serious literature. In more recent times, however, more emphasis has been placed on Thoma as a writer of exemplary prose. One critic of the early 1970s even calls Thoma "the greatest German prose writer in the twentieth century."[4] Recent interpreters from East Germany praise Thoma for portraying the Bavarian peasant as a socially useful individual who stands in sharp contrast to the "bourgeois, noble and intellectual parasites."[5]

Outside the German-speaking countries, just a few of Thoma's works have been known up to now. Only *Moral* has been translated into English. The predominant reason for the absence of further translations of his works is the near impossibility of adequately reproducing German dialect in a foreign language. Given the increasing interest in Thoma's novels—in which Bavarian dialect is used to a much lesser degree than in his comedies—within Germany, translation of some of his prose works may seem more probable in the future. In a period of nostalgic rediscovery of the time before World War I, Thoma's political satire might, hopefully, attract the interest of an ambitious translator.

Thoma's political views have been the subject of heated discussions in the past. His critics saw him as an irresponsible ultraliberal mocker on the one hand, and called him a dangerous reactionary on the other. Neither of these classifications gives a true account of his political convictions. If one wants to give a fair and just picture of Thoma as a *homo politicus,* his strong sense of truth and his irascible nature have to be taken into account. During the last two decades of the Second German Empire, when careless statements made by the rather blundering Wilhelm II became a frequent embarrassment for the country, and when press censorship increasingly threatened any form of constructive criticism, it was only natural for Thoma to find himself on the liberal side of the political spectrum. However, he never was an advocate of radical socialism or communism. Even during his imprisonment, it never occurred to him that anyone could want the destruction of the prevailing regime in Germany. It was pettiness and narrow-mindedness, whether in government or in the churches, that he vigorously opposed. When World War I broke out, he even forgot these points of disagreement, and the preservation of the German fatherland remained his only concern, as it did for so many other former critics of the regime. These same feelings and aims led Thoma to write articles for the *Miesbacher Anzeiger* during the difficult times after the war.

Ludwig Thoma preferred to be seen as a crude, no-nonsense Old Bavarian, somebody on whom one does not play tricks. This picture was conveniently enhanced by his coarse appearance and his standoffish bearing. However, he projected this image only toward people who did not know him or whom he did not want to know. Toward his friends and good acquaintances, he was very kind and sensitive. Josef Hofmiller, who enjoyed Thoma's acquaintance and trust during the last few years of the author's life, was able to set the record straight: beneath the rough outside there was a warm, sentimental core, and a heart that was easily hurt. This also explains Thoma's brusque behavior in public, and it makes one understand his profound desperation in Germany's dark years during and after World War I. Thoma never wanted to hurt anybody intentionally with his satires. He wanted to improve, teach, and help his country to find the right path into the future. "To feel internationally minded, to be fair against the fiercest enemies, was never in my nature, and it really was not at all difficult for me to wish destruction to them and a full victory to Germany. . . ." These remarks at the end of his autobiographical essay expose Thoma's honest and uncomplicated approach to the problem of the war.[6] One should understand this sentence in his autobiography as an expression of genuine sentiments, and as nothing more, or less. Because the existence of his country was at stake, Thoma resorted to writing patriotic pamphlets at the end of his life, because it was for his homeland and its people that he had become a writer in the first place.

Thoma's strong love for country and home was deeply rooted in his soul, and the cornerstone for his great affection had been laid in his childhood years when he first learned the meaning of *Heimat*. In his last years, established as the *poeta Bavariae*, Thoma revealed the secret of his life and work in two sentences, which may stand at the end of this book: "Many wishes I had were fulfilled, differently and more beautifully than I had expected, among them the wish which is rooted most deeply in me: to be allowed to live and work here. The closer the circle [of my life] draws itself, from the beginning to the end, the more I feel how the greatest happiness is enclosed in it. Around me is *Heimat*. . . ."[7]

Notes and References

Chapter One

1. *Cf. Ludwig Thoma, Gesammelte Werke.* New, enlarged edition. 6 vols. (Munich, 1968), vol. 1, p. 59f. This edition of Thoma's *Collected Works* is the most recent and reliable available to date. Quotations and references in this study are based on it.
2. *Ibid.*, p. 72f.
3. *Ibid.*, p. 53.
4. *Ibid.*, p. 94.
5. *Ibid.*, p. 131.
6. *Ibid.*, p. 96.
7. Anton Keller, ed. *Ludwig Thoma, Ein Leben in Briefen* (Munich, 1963), p. 14. Letter dated Aschaffenburg, December 4, 1886.
8. *Ibid.*, pp. 19 - 20. Letter dated Traunstein, August 9, 1887.
9,. *Gesammelte Werke*, vol. 1, p. 136.
10. *Ibid.*
11. *Ibid.*, p. 138.
12. *Ibid.*, p. 140.
13. *Ibid.*, p. 147.
14. *Ibid.*, p. 148.
15. *Ibid.*, p. 154.
16. *Ibid.*, p. 155.
17. *Ibid.*, p. 163.
18. *Ibid.*, p. 248.
19. *Ibid.*, p. 172f.
20. *Ibid.*, p. 176.
21. *Ibid.*, p. 177 - 78.
22. *Ibid.*, p. 178.
23. *Ein Leben in Briefen*, p. 341ff.
24. *Gesammelte Werke*, vol. 1, p. 183.
25. *Ein Leben in Briefen*, p. 82. Letter dated Munich, July 4, 1901.
26. *Gesammelte Werke*, vol. 1, p. 202.
27. *Ibid.*, p. 192.
28. *Ibid.*, p. 266.
29. *Ibid.*, p. 212.
30. *Ibid.*, p. 213.
31. *Ibid.*, vol. 4, pp. 174 - 81.
32. *Ein Leben in Briefen*, p. 338. Letter dated August 23, 1918.

33. *Ibid.*, p. 202. Letter dated Rissersee-Garmisch, January 21, 1908.
34. *Ibid.*
35. *Gesammelte Werke*, vol. 1, p. 255.
36. *Ein Leben in Briefen*, pp. 215 - 16. Letter dated Rottach, May 17, 1909.
37. *Ibid.*, p. 277. Letter dated Rottach, November 16, 1910.
38. *Ibid.*, p. 255. Letter dated Rottach, December 1, 1913.
39. *Ibid.*, p. 266. Letter dated Rottach, August 4, 1914 (to Theodor Heuss).
40. *Ibid.*, pp. 266 - 67. Letter dated Rottach, August 7, 1914.
41. *Ibid.*, pp. 379 - 80. Letter dated Rottach, August 11, 1919.
42. *Ibid.*, p. 345f. Letter dated Rottach, January 1, 1919.
43. *Ibid.*, p. 404. Letter dated Rottach, November 27, 1919.
44. Cf. Fritz Heinle, *Ludwig Thoma in Selbstzeugnissen und Bilddokumenten* (Reinbek bei Hamburg, 1963), p. 136.
45. *Ein Leben in Briefen*, 377. Letter dated Rottach, August 6, 1919.
46. *Ibid.*, p. 341. Letter dated Rottach, December 13, 1918.
47. *Ibid.*, p. 348. Letter dated January 2, 1919.
48. *Ibid.*, p. 390. Letter dated September 15, 1919.
49. *Ibid.*, p. 449. Letter dated April 11, 1921.
50. *Ibid.*, p. 454. Letter dated Rottach, May 12, 1921.
51. *Ibid.*, p. 456. Letter dated May 13, 1921.
52. *Ibid.*, p. 461. Letter dated August 5, 1921.
53. *Ibid.*, p. 463. Letter dated August 25, 1921.

Chapter Two

1. *Ein Leben in Briefen.*, p. 86. Letter dated Munich, August 28, 1901.
2. *Gesammelte Werke*, vol. 2, p. 231.
3. *Ibid.*, pp. 226 - 27.
4. *Ibid.*, p. 228.
5. *Ein Leben in Briefen*, p. 137. Letter dated Munich, October 21, 1902.
6. *Ibid.*, p. 140. Letter dated Munich, November 6, 1902.
7. Cf. p. 83f.
8. Cf. p. 91f.
9. *Gesammelte Werke*, vol. 2, p. 310.
10. *Ein Leben in Briefen*, p. 204. Letter dated Rottach, June 27, 1908.
11. *Ibid.*, p. 206. Letter dated Tuften, July 20, 1908.
12. *Ibid.*, p. 207. Letter dated Rottach, July 9, 1908.
13. *Ibid.*, pp. 207 - 08. Letter dated Rottach, September 12, 1908.
14. *Gesammelte Werke*, vol. 2, p. 651.
15. *Ein Leben in Briefen*, pp. 210 - 11. Letter dated Rottach, Tuften, October 21, 1908.
16. *Gesammelte Werke*, vol. 2, p. 382.
17. *Ibid.*

18. *Ein Leben in Briefen*, p. 226. Letter dated Rottach, August 7, 1910.
19. *Ibid.*, pp. 226 - 27. Letter dated Rottach, August 7, 1910.
20. Cf. *Gesammelte Werke*, vol. 2, p. 652.
21. *Ibid.*, vol. 1, p. 140.
22. *Ibid.*, p. 470.
23. *Ein Leben in Briefen*, p. 239. Letter dated Rottach, November 20, 1911.
24. *Ibid.*, p. 240. Letter dated Rottach, November 22, 1911 (to Carl Rössler).
25. *Ibid.* Letter dated Rottach, November 27, 1911.
26. *Ibid.*, p. 246. Letter dated Rottach, April 6, 1912.
27. *Ibid.*, p. 244. Letter dated Rottach, February 25, 1912.
28. *Ibid.*, p. 245. Letter dated Rottach, April 3, 1912 (to Conrad Haussmann).
29. *Ibid.*, pp. 245 - 46.
30. *Ibid.*, p. 250. Letter dated Rottach, December 24, 1912.

Chapter Three

1. *Ein Leben in Briefen*, p. 161. letter dated October 25, 1904.
2. Cf. Albert Soergel / Curt Hohoff, *Dichtung und Dichter der Zeit. Vom Naturalismus bis zur Gegenwart.* 2 vols. (Düsseldorf, 1961), vol 1, p. 648.
3. *Ein Leben in Briefen*, p. 228. Letter dated Rottach, January 25, 1911 (to Conrad Haussmann).
4. Cf. Soergel / Hohoff, *Dichtung und Dichter der Zeit*, vol. 1, p. 648.
5. *Ibid.*
6. Cf. *Ein Leben in Briefen*, pp. 452 - 53.
7. *Ibid.*, p. 452. Letter dated Rottach, April 19, 1921.
8. *Gesammelte Werke*, vol. 5, p. 23.
9. Cf. *Ein Leben in Briefen*, p. 317.
10. Cf. *ibid.*, p. 317.
11. Cf. *ibid.*, p. 400.
12. Cf. *ibid.*, p. 397.
13. *Ibid.*, p. 405. Letter dated Rottach, November 30, 1919.
14. Fritz Heinle, *Ludwig Thoma in Selbstzeugnissen und Bilddokumenten*, p. 138.

Chapter Four

1. *Gesammelte Werke*, vol. 4, p. 21.
2. *Ibid.*, p. 403.
3. Cf. Soergel / Hohoff, *Dichtung und Dichter der Zeit*, vol. 2, p. 647; and Fritz Heinle, *Ludwig Thoma in Selbstzeugnissen und Bilddokumenten*, p. 109.
4. Cf. *Gesammelte Werke*, vol. 4, pp. 147 - 395.

5. Cf. *ibid.*, p. 669.
6. Cf. *ibid.*, pp. 161 - 63.
7. Cf. *ibid.*, pp. 261 - 64.
8. In 1900 the German Reich sent troops to China (as did several other major powers) in order to crush the Boxer Rebellion.
9. Cf. *Gesammelte Werke*, vol. 4, pp. 571 - 73.
10. Cf. *ibid.*, vol. 6, p. 661.
11. *Ibid.*, p. 686.
12. *Ibid.*, p. 718.
13. *Ibid.*, p. 719.
14. *Ibid.*
15. *Ibid.*, pp. 713 - 14.

Chapter Five

1. *Ein Leben in Briefen*, p. 386. Letter dated Rottach, August 31, 1919.
2. *Ibid.*, p. 390. Letter dated Rottach, September 15, 1919.
3. Cf. *Gesammelte Werke*, vol. 3, p. 235ff.
4. Cf. Heinrich Meyer, *Die Kunst des Erzählens* (Bern, Munich, 1972), p. 143.
5. Cf. Hans Kaufmann / Sylvia Schlenstedt, ed., *Geschichte der deutschen Literatur* (Berlin, 1974), vol. 9, p. 128.
6. Cf. *ibid.*, vol. 1, p. 230.
7. *Ibid.*, p. 231.

Selected Bibliography

PRIMARY SOURCES

Gesammelte Werke. New, enlarged ed. 6 vols. Munich: Piper, 1968. Standard edition.

Ausgewählte Werke. 3 vols. With a preface by Eugen Roth. Munich: Piper, 1966.

Ausgewählte Werke. 1 vol. With a preface by Eugen Roth. Munich: Piper, 1966. Brief and handy.

Cora; vier Lausbubengeschichten. Edited by William Diamond and Selma Rosenfeld. New edition Boston: Heath, 1961. Original edition Chicago: The University of Chicago Press, 1933. Brief introduction.

Die Lokalbahn. Edited with introduction, notes and vocabulary by A. E. Zucker. New York: F. S. Crofts, 1931.

Moral; a Comedy in Three Acts, translated by Charles Recht. New York: Knopf, 1916. Brief introduction.

SECONDARY SOURCES

1. Biographical

GRAF, OSKAR M. "Dem Gedenken Ludwig Thomas." *An manchen Tagen. Reden, Gedanken und Zeitabhandlungen*. Frankfurt | Main: Nest Verlag, 1961, 48 - 75. Speech held before the German Departments of Princeton, Johns Hopkins and Maryland Universities, 1944.

HAAGE, PETER, *Mit Nagelstiefeln durchs Kaiserreich. Ludwig Thoma. Eine Biographie*. Munich, Gütersloh, Vienna: Bertelsmann, 1975. Easy to read biography. No bibliography.

HOFMILLER, JOSEPH1, "HERBSTTAGE MIT LUDWIG THOMA." *Bayernbüchlein*. Munich: Langen / Müller, 1942, 3 - 10. Moving account of a visit with Thoma shortly before his death.

HOLM, KORFIZ, "Ludwig Thoma, wie ich ihn erlebte." *Das innere Reich*, 3, II (1936 - 37), 1268 - 83. Account of the friendship between Thoma and Korfiz Holm. Written on the occasion of the seventieth anniversary of Thoma's birth.

KELLER, ANTON, ED. *Ludwig Thoma,. Ein leben in Briefen*. Munich: Piper, 1963.

LEMP, RICHARD, ed. *Eine bayerische Freundschaft in Briefen / Ludwig Thoma, Ignatius Taschner*. Reinbek bei Hamburg: Rowohlt, 1973. Correspondence with Taschner (illustrated).

LIEBERMANN, MAIDI VON, "Erinnerungen an Ludwig Thoma.," *Bayerland*, 56 (1954), 188 - 90.

ROTH, ADOLF, "Ludwig Thomas Vorfahren." *Familie und Volk*, 2 (1953), 369 - 74. History of Thoma's ancestry.

ROTHMAIER, RICHARD, *Mein Freund Ludwig Thoma*. Edited by Friedl Brehm. Altötting: Coppenrath, 1949.

SCHULTES, BERTL, *Ein Komödiant blickt zurück. Erinnerungen an Ludwig Thoma, das Bauerntheater und deren Freunde.* Munich: Feder Verlag, 1963.

SIEGHARDT, AUGUST, "Ludwig Thomas oberpfälzische Abstammung. Neue Forchungsergebnisse." *Oberpfalz*, 44 (1956), 179 - 80.

THUMSER, GERD, ed. *Anekdoten um Ludwig Thoma*. Munich, Esslingen: Bechtle, 1968. A collection of anecdotes.

ZIERSCH, WALTHER, *Ludwig Thoma und die Münchner Stadt*. Mit einer Handschrift von Ludwig Thoma. Gauting: Bavaria Verlag, 1936. Highly personal biographical account.

2. Critical Studies

BAUER, JOSEF MARTIN, "Thoma contra Ruederer." *Unbekanntes Bayern*, 6 (1961), 225 - 41.

BEYSCHLAG, SIEGFRIED, "Ludwig Thomas Romandichtung." *Euphorion*, 47 (1953), 79 - 96. Analysis of Thoma's novels.

BOESCHENSTEIN, HERMANN, "Zu Ludwig Thomas 'Andreas Vöst'." *Germanic Review*, 11 (1936), 207 - 13. An interpretation of Thoma's first novel.

BREHM, FRIEDL, *Ludwig Thoma und der Simplicissimus. Immer gegen die Machthaber.* Feldafing: Brehm, 1966. Very brief description of Thoma's relation to the *Simplicissimus*. Short bibliography.

————. *Sehnsucht nach Unterdrückung. Zensur und Presserecht bei Ludwig Thoma.* Feldafing: Brehm, 1957.

————. *Zehn haben neun Meinungen. Kritik und Kritiker bei Ludwig Thoma.* Feldafing: Brehm, 1958.

DIAMOND, WILLIAM, "Ludwig Thoma." *Monatshefte*, 21 (1929), 97 - 101. Short assessment of Thoma's works.

DREWS, ARTHUR, "Ludwig Thoma." *Preussische Jahrbücher*, 178 (1919), 340 - 45.

GLUTH, OSKAR, "Ludwig Thoma." *Deutsches biographisches Jahrbuch*, 3 (1921), 257 - 63. Stuttgart: Deutsche Verlags-Anstalt, 1927.

GRUN, BERNHARD, "Ludwig Thoma und Karl Valentin." In: B. G., *Aller Spass dieser Welt*. Frankfurt / Main: A. Langen, 1966, 325 - 31. Very short characterization of Thoma and his work.

HEILBRONNER, WALTER L. "Ludwig Thoma as a Social and Political Critic and Satirist." Diss. Ann Arbor, Univ. Microfilms, Publ. No. 12, 584, 1955. Interesting account of Thoma's political stance.

————. "A Reappraisal of Ludwig Thoma." *German Quarterly*, 30 (1957), 247 - 53. On Thoma's political views.

HEINLE, FRITZ, *Ludwig Thoma in Selbstzeugnissen und Bilddokumenten.* Reinbek bei Hamburg: Rowohlt, 1963. A study on Thoma's life and works.

HEISELER, BERNT VON, "Ludwig Thoma, der Dichter." *Die Sammlung,* 22 (1957), 25 - 32.

KAUFMANN, HANS, "Fortsetzung realistischer Erzähltraditionen des 19. Jahrhunderts bei Ludwig Thoma, A. Schnitzler, E. v. Keyserling, G., Hauptmann und dem frühen Hermann Hesse." *Wissenschaftliche Zeitschrift der Friedrich-Schiller-Universität Jena. Gesellschafts-und sprachwissenschaftliche Reihe,* 20 (1971), 499 - 512. Thoma is seen as a critic of the bourgeoisie and the clergy.

PEUKERT, WILL-ERICH, "Ludwig Thoma." *Zeitschrift für deutsche Philologie,* 71 (1951 - 52), 369 - 73. Folkloristic and sociological aspects of Thoma and his work.

RICHARDI, HANS GÜNTHER, *Ludwig Thoma und die Dachauer Lokalbahn.* Dachau: Gerhard Winkler, 1974.

RONDE, GERTRUD, "Die Mundart Ludwig Thomas." *Schönere Heimat,* 56 (1967), 61 - 67.

SANDROCK, JAMES P. *Ludwig Thoma: Aspects of his Art.* Göppingen: A. Kümmerle, 1975, A critical study using the topical approach.

SCHNEIDER, LUDWIG, "Ludwig Thoma. Versuch einer geistesgeschichtlichen Einordnung." *Weltstimmen,* 22 (1953), 342 - 49. Emphasis is placed on Thoma's close relationship to his region and its impact on his thinking.

THUMSER, GERD, *Ludwig Thoma und seine Welt.* Munich: Verlag Kurt Desch, 1966.

WHITE, D. V., "Ludwig Thoma as a Political Satirist." *German Life and Letters,* 13 (1959 - 60), 214 - 19. An interpretation of the *Filser Letters.*

ZIERSCH, ROLAND, *Ludwig Thoma.* Mühlacker: Stieglitz Verlag, 1964.

Index

(The works of Thoma are listed under his name)

152